To Brian and Julia
for a life enriched by beauty

David and Reba Uttewsky
8-29-92

THE KREMLIN
AND ITS TREASURES

THE KREMLIN
AND ITS TREASURES

Irina Rodimzeva

Nikolai Rachmanov

Alfons Raimann

Rizzoli
NEW YORK

First published in the United States of America in 1987 by
RIZZOLI INTERNATIONAL PUBLICATIONS, INC.
597 Fifth Avenue, New York, NY 10017

Copyright © 1986 Desertina Verlag, Disentis/Muster, Switzerland
This edition was realized through Motovun (Switzerland) Copublishing
Company Ltd., Lucerne

Library of Congress Cataloging-in-Publication Data

Rodimzeva, Irina, 1934–
    The Kremlin and its art treasures.

    Bibliography: p.
    Includes index.
    1. Kremlin (Moscow, R.S.R.S.R.),   2. Art, Russian –
Russian S.F.S.R. – Moscow.   3. Art – Russian S.F.S.R. –
Moscow.   I. Rachmanov, Nicolai, 1932 –
II. Raimann, Alfons.   III. Title.
N6997.M7R6 1987   708.7'312   87 – 45383
ISBN 0-8478-0856-4

Translation: Catherine Badger
Text: Irina Rodimzeva
Illustrations: Nikolai Rachmanov
Planning and Editing: Alfons Raimann
Design: Roger Tschopp, Condrau SA
Cover Design: Hildebrand Bernet
Production: Stampa Romontscha Condrau SA, Disentis/Muster
Photolithographs: Mengis + Sticher AG, Lucerne
Paper: Papierfabriken Cham Tenero SA
Binding: Burkhardt AG, Mönchaltorf

Printed and bound in Switzerland

Table of Contents

Foreword

This magnificent art book is a noteworthy cultural event which I am convinced will shed new light on the Kremlin for its readers. Unique collections and masterpieces of art from European and Eastern countries spanning a period of 15 centuries are covered in this volume.

The Moscow Kremlin is presented as a majestic ensemble of outstanding Russian architecture from six centuries. Buildings from about 1500 A.D. form the heart of this complex: the Uspenskii (Assumption) Cathedral, the Blagoveshchenskii (Annunciation) Cathedral, the Archangel Cathedral, the Church of the Repository of the Robe, the Palace of Facets, the Belfry of Ivan the Great, the Kremlin Wall, and the towers. They symbolize the development of a central Russian state under the leadership of Moscow. Each of these monuments, as well as the complex as a whole, testify to the Russian people's great architecture and desire for art. At the same time, they all result from the fruitful cooperation between Russian and Western European artists and artisans. The palaces dating from the 17th to the 19th centuries also are impressive and valuable for art historians: Terem Palace, the Patriarchal Palace and the Church of the Twelve Apostles, the Arsenal, the Senate Building, and the Grand Kremlin Palace.

Shortly after the Great Revolution in 1917, Moscow became the capital and the Kremlin, the political and cultural center of the Soviet Union. The seats of government and parliament (the Supreme Soviet of the USSR) have been located here since 1918. Vladimir Ulyanov (Lenin), whose private and working chambers have been carefully transformed into a well-kept memorial, lived and worked here. The Building of the Presidium of the Supreme Soviet of the USSR and the Palace of Congress, built in the 1930s and early 1960s, were integrated into the architectural style of the Kremlin. Here, events took place that were of enormous importance for the Soviet Union.

The Kremlin museums' art collections were established in several ways over many centuries. Russian artists and artisans created a significant part of the art and crafts works in the numerous Kremlin workshops for the tsarist and patriarchal courts. Frequently they were directly motivated by decisive events in the life of the Russian people and state. Because these works reflect such happenings, they figure significantly in historical research.

Over the centuries, the most valuable old Russian works of art from various principalities and cities, as well as rare, precious Western European and Eastern jewelry, accumulated in the Kremlin cathedrals and the treasuries of the grand princes and metropolitans. As of the 14th century, the treasures of the Grand Prince of Moscow were hereditary, and their total value increased by the addition of outstanding works of following generations.

Russia's diplomatic and economic ties throughout the world provided a further source for the collections. Ambassadors to Russia, whose custom it was to bring gifts from their monarchs in Western Europe and the East, contributed to the accumulation of fantastic riches in the rooms and chests of the Treasury of the Grand Prince. Slowly, complete collections of different foreign and local schools of art and styles were built up in this manner. One feature of the Kremlin collections is their inclusion of nearly every type and school of art: icon and fresco painting, jewelry, wood sculpture, masonry, arms manufacture, carriage building, casting, etc. The Kremlin collections provide an overall view of all important developments in Russian art and a reliable account of Russian culture.

In order to aid the reader in finding his way through the treasures of the Kremlin, ten significant complexes of which the museums are especially proud have been selected from their entire range.

1. The collection of old Russian paintings from the 11th to the 18th centuries. It includes the fresco and icon collections of the Cathedrals of the Assumption, the Annunciation, and the Archangel, the Church of the Repository of the Robe, and the court chapels and palaces. Represented are all the leading Russian centers of art – Novgorod, Pskov, Vladimir, Moscow, the northern Russian monasteries in Solovetskii and Kirill-Belozersk –

as well as icon paintings from Byzantium and the southern Slavic countries. Works by Andrei Rublev, Theophanes the Greek, Dionissius, and the famed masters of the 17th century (Simon Ushakov, Feodor Subov, Tichon Philatyev, Nazari Istomin) are highlights.

2. The largest collection of Russian, Western European, and Eastern parade and hunting weapons and armor from the 13th to the 19th centuries. It includes the unique collection of cannons from the 16th and 17th centuries, to which artillery from all Western European countries, in addition to the well-known Tsar Cannon, belong.

3. The largest Soviet collection of Russian gold and silver jewelry (from the 12th to the beginning of the 20th century) with true masterpieces of supreme historical and artistic value. Only the Kremlin collection can provide a comprehensive view of the development of Russian jewelry, because it embraces works from masters of all the centers and schools of art.

4. The unsurpassed collection of Western European silver work (from the 16th to the 19th century). It is founded on gifts that ambassadors brought from the monarchs of England, Germany, Austria, Sweden, Denmark, Holland, Poland, and other countries, as well as on generous donations by ambassadors and merchants, which all testify to Russia's far-reaching political, economic, and cultural ties.

5. The unique collection of church vestments decorated with gold and silver embroidery, pearls, and precious stones, and of secular clothing sewn of old, valuable textiles dating from the 14th to the beginning of the 20th century. Handmade fabrics from Byzantium, Iran, Turkey, China, Italy, France, Spain, and Russia are represented here.

6. The collection of gala riding habits from the 16th to the 19th century, created by masters from Russia, Persia, Turkey, Rumania, Poland, China, and Bukhara. This collection is unequaled in the world.

7. The collection of state insignia, crowns, imperial crowns, thrones, scepters, imperial orbs, and coronation robes from the 16th to the 19th century, which is of great historical and artistic value.

8. The collection of carriages and coaches from Russia and Western European countries (from the 16th to the second half of the 18th century). It is considered to be the world's richest.

9. The collection of Russian, Western European, and Eastern glass and porcelain artworks (from the 17th to the beginning of the 20th century).

10. The coin collection (from the 11th to the beginning of the 20th century).

The Kremlin registers the highest number of visitors among museums in the Soviet Union: four and a half million annually, including about one million foreign tourists. Each year, over 20 million people visit the Moscow Kremlin. The Kremlin collections are constantly being enlarged with further precious objects obtained from collectors or antique shops, donated by private persons, or discovered in archaeological explorations on the Kremlin site. During the years of Soviet rule, the number of exhibits in all collections in the Kremlin museums has more than doubled.

One of the museums' most important tasks is to preserve this inheritance for coming generations. This was stated explicitly in one of the first decrees of the Soviet government. The law for the protection and use of cultural and historical monuments passed on October 28, 1976, by the Supreme Soviet of the USSR serves the same purpose. It is only natural that the monuments of the Kremlin should be accorded special attention by the Soviet nation. More comprehensive and varied preservation and restoration programs have been carried out over the last two decades than in the entire history of the Moscow Kremlin. As a part of these programs, the walls, towers, cathedrals, and other old Kremlin buildings have been completely restored and preserved structurally. Most important, the durability of these monuments was ensured by stabilizing them in whole and in part. The chief goal of the restoration consisted in reestablishing the original architecture of many monuments, a process which has brought out the uniqueness of a number of them. At the same time, the contemporary conception of the architectural ensemble of the Moscow Kremlin as a unified composition was to be more sharply defined and perfected. Each restored object required the development of individualized methods for surface treatment, coloration, and preservation. Among others, these methods included preventing corrosion by securing copper sheets to the domes without damaging the layers of gilt and protecting stonework from microorganisms. Soviet and international knowledge in restoration and engineering, as well as achievements in modern science and technology, were thus applied ex-

tensively. A team of highly qualified architects, archaeologists, historians, and art historians conducted a thorough investigation of the entire site and all Kremlin structures, thus making it possible to save valuable frescos from the 15th to the 17th century, a part of the international cultural heritage. The museums' collections could also be enriched by the addition of many archaeological finds; the study of art, by discoveries in the fields of architecture and painting.

Renovation and restoration work in the Kremlin is approaching completion. Attention is now being turned toward the organization and presentation of new exhibitions.

M. Zukanov
Director of the National Museums
of the Moscow Kremlin

ON THE HISTORY OF THE KREMLIN

The Unknown Past

The approximately 800-year-old history of the Moscow Kremlin provides a unique chronicle of the Russian state and culture.

The area in which Moscow is located must have attracted people very early. The oldest settlements can be dated back to over 5000 years ago, when fishers and hunters built light, leaf-covered huts on the densely wooded shores and riverbanks. Thus, archaeologists today attribute the extended camp near Lyalovo (in Greater Moscow) to the Late Stone Age. The so-called Fatyanovo civilization dates back to the Bronze Age: in Fatyanovo village, carefully honed axes and women's bronze jewelry, as well as bear-tooth and bear-bone necklaces, were uncovered in a burial site.

During the Ice Age, the dense forests on the Moskva River must already have sheltered many *gorodishche*, small fortified settlements usually surrounded by moats and earthen embankments, often augmented by a palisade. Best suited for such a settlement was a steep riverbank or, even better, a headland between two rivers or river arms, which provided natural protection against enemy attacks. The settlers lived chiefly from stock-raising and farming. Also, they were already able to produce iron from bog iron ores smelted in pots and crucibles. Sickles, knives, and arrowheads were made from the iron, whereas bronze and silver were used for women's jewelry even then. According to archaeological classification, this type of settlement belongs to the Dyakovo civilization, named for a settlement in Kolomenskoye, now a part of Moscow.

At the end of the 11th and during the first half of the 12th century A. D., the Kriwichi, a tribe of North Slovenians from the Novgorod area, settled in the area north of the Moskva, while the East Slav tribe of the Vyatichi settled in the southern part of the future Moscow. Both tribes farmed and were more advanced culturally than the Dyakovo civilization. At that early date, a tribal nobility began to develop. Thus, Moscow arose on the border between two Slavic tribes.

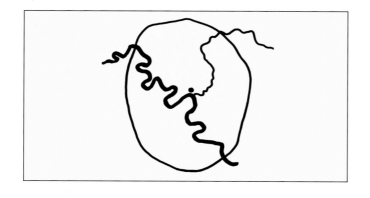

◁ Present-day Moscow city area (oval area) showing the Moskva (thick line) and Yauza Rivers and the Kremlin, the origin and core of the settlement.

▷ △ Copper and bronze jewelry from excavations in the Moscow area. The rings are made of a glass-like material.

▷ The sculptured bust of a woman from the Bronze Age. Reconstruction by M. Gerassimov.

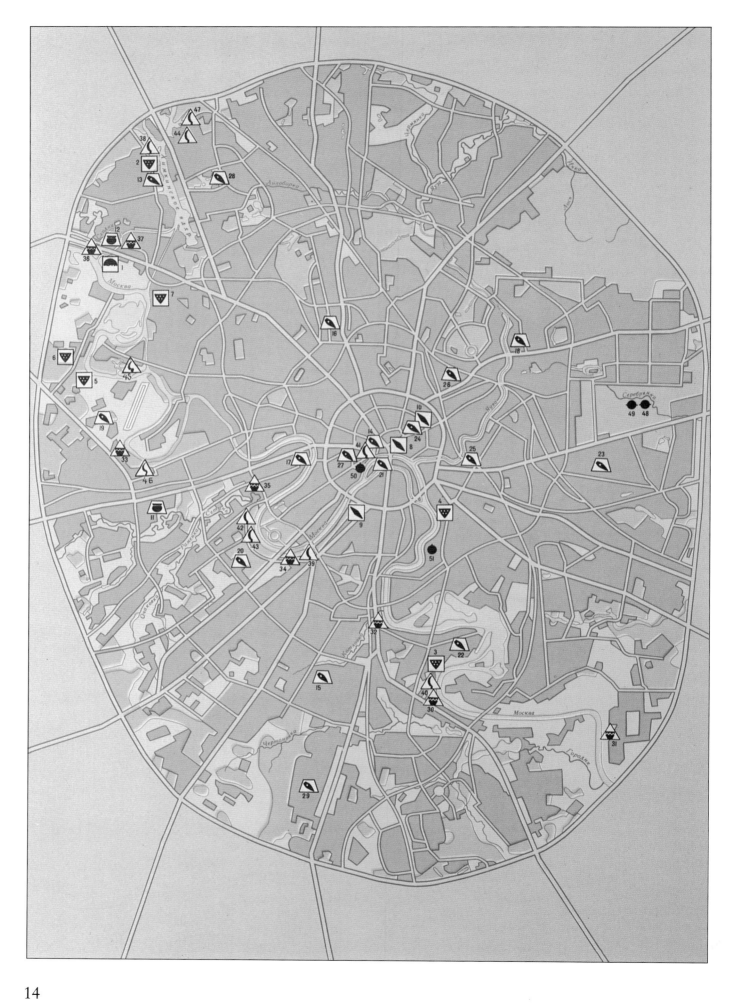

△ Mug and mythical animal, two particularly interesting objects among the rich archaeological finds in the Moscow area.

◁ Diagram of finds from ancient cultures in the Moscow area.

I. Stone Age
🔲 Cranium of Paleolithic person
1. Mouth of the Shodnia River

🔳 Neolithic locations
2. Aleshkinskaia; 3. Dyakovskaia; 4. Krutitskaia;
5. Zerebryanoborskaia; 6. Troitselykovskaia;
7. Shukovskaia

🔳 Location of individual finds from the Neolithic Age
8. Tsaryadye; 9. Gorky Park; 10. Pokrov Gate

II. Bronze Age
(Fatyanov civilization)

🔳 Burial sites
11. Davydovski; 12. Tuzinki

🔳 Location of individual finds from the Bronze Age
13. Aleshkino; 14. Kremlin; 15. Tsiutsino; 16. Butyr
Court; Dorogomilovo; 18. Tselyev; 19. Krylatskoya;
20. Lenin Hills; 21. Moriza Toretsa Quai; 22. Nago-

tino; 23. Perovo; 24. Pokrov Gate; 25. Pryamikov
Square; 26. Rusakovskaia Street; 27. Zivtsev Vrashek;
28. Khimki-Khovrino; 29. Chertanovo

III. Early Iron Age
(Dyakov civilization)

🔳 Prehistoric settlements
30. Dyakovskoye; 31. Kapotinskoye; 32. Lower
Kotlovshe; 33. Kuntsevskoye; 34. Mamontovo;
35. Zetunskoye; 36. Spas-Tushinskoye;
37. Tushinskoye

🔳 Early settlements
38. Aleshkinskoye; 39. Andreyevskoye;
40. Dyakovskoye; 41. Kremlevskoye; 42./43. Lenin
Hills; 44. Nikolskoye; 45. Tatarovskoye;
46. Philevskoye; 47. Khimkinskoye

● Finding-places of old coins
48. Itsmaylovo. Parphian coins, 2nd century B.C.;
49. Itsmaylovo. Roman coins, 3rd century B.C.;
50. Kropotkin Quai, 9th century A.D.; 51. Lenin
Village (near the former Simonov Monastery),
9th century A.D.

The First Mention of Moscow

The name of Moscow first appeared in documents over eight centuries ago. On the western border of the Suzdal principality was a fortified settlement on a high hill covered with pine woods, around which the Moskva and Neglinnaia Rivers flowed. It must have been founded at the end of the 11th century. Recent archaeological investigations on Borovitskii Hill have uncovered the remains of buildings, fortifications and street pavements from that time. The hill, whose name is derived from *borovitse* (pine) is still the highest elevation on the Kremlin site.

A chronicle dated 1147 contains a fascinating account of Iurii, Prince of Suzdal and the son of Vladimir Monomakh. After a campaign against Novgorod, Iurii, known for his hotheadedness and called Dolgorukii (the Long-Armed) by the people, invited his ally and relative Svyatoslav Olgovich, Prince of Novgorod-Segverskii, to visit him, saying "visit me, brother, in Moscow." The chronicler reports that a council of war was held in Moscow and the participants dined "abundantly and with pleasure." This year, when Moscow was first mentioned in a Russian chronicle, is regarded as the official date of its founding.

Annalists and historians have always wanted to know more precisely when and how this city, destined to play an extraordinary role, really arose. Therefore they have also studied reports of a more legendary nature. The "Saga of the Origin of Moscow" probably contains a kernel of truth. According to that tale, Iurii Dolgorukii stopped to rest on his journey from Kiev to Vladimir in a domain belonging to the boyar Kuchko Ivanovich. However, the arrogant nobleman did not show the Prince of Suzdal the proper respect, for which he paid with his life. Dolgorukii had the boyar's sons raised at his court, and Kuchko's beautiful daughter was married to Andrei, the Prince's son. On the site of the murdered boyar's village, Prince Iurii established a city that was named after the adjoining river (the Moskva). Unfortunately, the legend has an evil ending: Kuchko's sons avenged their father by murdering their sister and her husband. M. N. Karamsin, the noted Russian historian from the 19th century, did not believe this legend, since there is no mention of a boyar named Kuchko in any of the documents. Despite this, these events seem credible, even in the light of modern historical research. The Kuchkovichi (sons of Kuchko), as well as Kuchko's son-in-law Peter, are mentioned in the chronicles. Furthermore, the fact that Andrei Bogolubski was murdered by his immediate relatives ist also verified by the documents.

Thus, the name of the future Russian capital derives from the river and not, as was often the case with village names, from the name of a prince. In records dating from the second half of the 12th century, Moscow is also sometimes called Kuchkovo, supporting an argu-

△ Illustration for the first mention of Moscow in the chronicles. Depicts the meeting of Prince Iurii Dolgorukii of Suzdal with Prince Svyatoslav Olgovich in Moscow on April 4, 1147. Miniature from the 16th century.

ment for the truth of the gist of the legend. Prince Iurii Dolgorukii, a prudent man of action, had the further strongholds of Iuriev-Polskoi (1152) and Dmitrov (1154) built to protect his western border. Yet to Moscow fell the special role in the history of the Russian people, which was probably favored most by Moscow's location at the crossing of old trade routes.

17

The First Moscow Kremlin

As the years passed, the chroniclers increasingly had opportunity to report interesting news about Moscow. In a section dated 1156, the chronicle of Tver noted that Iurii Dolgorukii fortified the heart of the settlement – the Kremlin – with earthworks. During construction of the Palace of Congress in the Kremlin from 1956 to 1960, remains of the mid-12th-century fortifications were uncovered in the excavated area. Archaeologists and architects reconstructed a 700-meter-long, approximately 40-meter-wide and 8-meter-high earthen wall. The foundation of extremely exposed sections of the wall was formed by three rows of wooden timbers bound together with wooden cotters. On top of the rampart, a wall made of shaped timbers probably provided further protection. (Earlier researchers thought a palisade was located here.) There may also have been two or three wooden watchtowers.

The moats of older fortified settlements were probably refilled in the 12th century. At that time, the site on Borovitskii Hill was large enough for the Kremlin. Near the fortified estate of the prince was a settlement of traders and artisans that extended along the hill on the Moskva. The marketplace lay in front of the wall (where today Ivan Square and the Arsenal are located). The landing-place on the Moskva was also situated in the protected area. Not only was the Kremlin the prince's residence and a center of trade, but it also offered the inhabitants of the surrounding villages shelter when danger threatened. Trade and craftsmanship first flourished in Moscow toward the end of the 12th century. Economic ties to other cities and countries became increasingly numerous and stable. Glass bracelets (found during excavations in the Kremlin) came from Kiev, coins from Central Asia and Armenia, copper from Bulgarian tribes on the Volga, from the Caucausus came boxwood, which was used to make especially durable combs, and amphoras of wine and spices came from Hermones on the Black Sea. As time went by, the small fortress on the border became stronger and more influential. However, whenever rival princes went to war or enemies attacked the city, the peace and security of Moscow's inhabitants was disrupted. This is shown by the sporadic records from around the turn of the 13th century. In 1176, for example, Prince Gleb of Ryazan laid siege to the fortified settlement on the Moskva, captured it, and then burned it to the ground.

▷ Two early stages of the Moscow Kremlin. Above, Iurii Dolgorukii's fort (from the second half of the 12th century). Below, the expanded complex in the 13th century. Pictorial reconstruction by Alexander Wechsler (Moscow, around 1970).

Far away on the Mongolian steppe, Khan Batu's countless horses set out on their campaign against the West in 1237. On December 21 of that year, Ryazan was taken by storm. Since the Russian princes were occupied with carrying out their feuds with one another, the Batu army streamed into the interior. Even Moscow, with its wooden wall dating from the time of Iurii Dolgorukii, was unable to withstand the attack. Batu swept away all obstacles in his path as he advanced through feuding Russia like a prairie fire.

Moscow was repeatedly sacked and burned down by the Tatars over the following decades. Yet each time, the settlement reemerged from the smoking ruins stronger than before. During that period, the ethnic core of the great Russian people developed between the Volga and the Oka. Moscow gained considerably in importance when Alexander Nevski, Prince of Novgorod, declared Moscow a princedom for his youngest son, Daniil (1261–1303). The first stone structures were erected around that time.

The principality of Moscow rose against a background of bitter fighting for supremacy among the Russian states at the beginning of the 14th century. Motivated by the thought of independence, Moscow struggled to unite the small Russian princedoms in the fight against the Tatar yoke, yet its interests clashed with those of the Tver princedom. Although Tver was superior in size, the Muscovite princes proved to be politically more mature and prudent.

In 1318, Iurii Danilovich (ca. 1280–1325) was the first Muscovite prince to receive a *yarlik* (patent) awarding him the title of Grand Prince. This enabled the ruler of Moscow to use his influence to unite all Russian forces. Iurii Danilovich wanted to first secure the northern border, which he accomplished by signing a border treaty with Sweden. Yet his life was too short for him to continue his policy. In 1325 his rival, Prince Dmitrii of Tver, murdered him during a visit by the Tatar Horde.

Fortune was kinder to Iurii's brother, Prince Ivan Danilovich Kalita, who ruled from 1325 to 1340. He was considered a careful and efficient man in business matters. His Old Russian name, Kalita (Moneybag), was given him for good reason. In 1327 Ivan Kalita, allied with the Tatars, defeated an uprising against the Tatar ruler in Tver and was rewarded with a patent in which the Horde named him Grand Prince. From that time on, the Tatar *Baskasy* (collectors) ceased to collect the tributes for the Hordes, a task which was then assumed by Russian princes. Thus, the foundation of Moscow's future power was laid under Ivan Kalita.

▷ △ Excavation and exhibition of a log-cabin style structure discovered during construction of the Palace of Congress in 1956.

▷ The Kremlin and its first stone structures (first half of the 14th century). Pictorial reconstruction by Apolinari Vasnetsov (Moscow, 1922).

Of the utmost importance for the growing power of the principality was the removal of the seat of the Russian Church from Vladimir to Moscow by its head. As the richest, most powerful landowner, the Church was extremely interested in uniting the Russian forces and therefore supported the policies of the Muscovite potentates. Metropolitan Peter spent much time in Moscow, where he died in 1326 and was buried. The Church declared him the first miracle worker of Moscow and all of Russia, as well as the patron of the city. Under his successor, Feognost (d. 1352), Moscow finally became the residence of the patriarch of the Russian Church.

In the early 14th century, new quarters and suburbs sprang up in and around Moscow each year. Inside the Kremlin, imposing buildings were constructed of white stone: in 1326 the Cathedral of the Assumption was built according to the prototype in Vladimir; in 1333 the Cathedral of the Archangel, as the burial place for Muscovite princes; and in 1330 the Church of the Savior, as the prince's private chapel. The spire of the Church of Ivan Lestvichnik, built in 1329, stood out among the churches around present-day Cathedral Square. On the steep hillside, the princes' palaces dominated the appearance of the city. Ivan Kalita, who had a great sense of tradition, had new ecclesiastical buildings erected on the same sites on which churches or cathedrals had stood during his father's lifetime. Thus, the general character of the Kremlin complex developed during his reign, although the complex would be repeatedly altered and enlarged in later years.

Linguists and historians have studied the etymology of the word *kremlin* for a considerable time. The term first appears in the Tver chronicle in 1315. It has not yet been possible to definitively pinpoint its origin. At one time, a widespread opinion held that the name had a Greek root. However, several indicators point to a Slavic or Russian origin. During the Middle Ages Tver had its own *kremnik*. In northern Russia, the wood used for building was called *kremy*. Originally, the word probably meant "fort" or "citadel."

In 1331 and 1337, terrible fires destroyed the wall around the Kremlin, which was over 200 years old, as well as a large part ot the settlement. Moscow experienced a turbulent building boom during its reconstruction (1339–1340). A new wall of mighty oak timbers arose in only five months. When the Grand Kremlin Palace was built in the 19th century, remains of this 14th-century fortification were uncovered. The great timbers measured up to 70 centimeters in diameter (and can be seen today in the Historical Museum). As was typical of fortress construction in the 14th century, the wall was made of wooden box sections carpentered in log-cabin style, filled with earth and stones and joined to form huge structures. The length of the individual boxes (six to eight meters) depended on the timbers. The width

◁ Ecclesiastical document of Muscovite Prince Semyon Ivanovich, 1353 (Moscow National Archives).

was determined in such a way as to allow the defenders enough room to move about on top during battle.

The layout of the new 14th-century Kremlin also formed a triangle. It was protected on two sides by the Moskva and Neglinnaia Rivers and on the east flank by a moat and earthen wall that extended approximately from the present Middle Arsenal Tower to the Moskva. During Ivan Kalita's time, the Kremlin doubled in size. A part of the eastern settlement, Possad, was enclosed in the ring. About 30 years after its completion, the oak wall and towers also succumbed to fire: a catastrophic blaze broke out in the Church of All Saints during the hot, dry summer of 1365. All of Moscow burned to the ground within a few hours.

Whitestone Moscow

The Russian states' struggle for independence intensified noticeably towards the middle of the 14th century. During the reconstruction of Moscow after the fire of 1365, young Prince Dmitrii Ivanovich, the grandson of Ivan Kalita, felt compelled to enlarge the fortifications in order to repel attacks by the Golden Horde and the Lithuanians. He ordered the new walls built of stone to prevent further catastrophic fires. Throughout the winter of 1367, white sandstone was transported by sled to Moscow from the Myachikovo settlement 30 kilometers away so that construction of the wall could be started that spring. The new ring was located about 60 meters farther from the center than the previous wall and was probably about two to three meters thick. The Kremlin site thus extended in the northeast almost to the present border. Moats were dug in those places where streams or rivers did not provide a natural defense, which in turn led to the necessity for a system of drawbridges on the three gate towers, Konstantin Yelena, Frolov, and Nikolskaia. The battlements and all eight or nine towers had stone merlons and embrasures, and wooden "tent" roofs covered the towers. Some sources name as the architects the Russians Ivan Sobakin, Feodor Sviblov, and Feodor Beklemish, all of whom had estates within the Kremlin, but no proof of this claim exists.

The construction of a stone fortress was rare in northeastern Russia in the 14th century. Up until then, brick walls were to be found only in Novgorod and Pskov. The Moscow Kremlin was soon to experience its baptism by fire: in 1368 and 1370, Prince Olgerd of Lithuania attempted to force the city on the Moskva to its knees. Both times, surrounding villages were burnt down and their inhabitants taken prisoner. Yet the stone Kremlin proved impregnable for Olgerd, although the walls had not yet been completed.

In 1375, Prince Michail of Tver signed a peace treaty with Moscow, which was tantamount to recognizing the principality's superiority. The Golden Horde eyed Moscow's increasing power suspiciously, and a decisive battle was imminent. At the end of August 1380, a Russian army led by Prince Dmitrii marched to the upper Don, where the troops of the Tatar commander, Mamai, were waiting for their ally, Prince Vladislaus Yagailo of Lithuania. Before the enemy troops could unite, Dmitrii attacked them on Kulikovo Pole (Field of Woodcocks) on September 8. The Khan tried to escape to the Crimea but was killed while fleeing. The Golden Horde, which had terrorized all of West Europe for over a century and a half, never recovered from this defeat, and the victory strengthened the Russian sense of nationality. Songs, sagas, and legends told of the great deeds of Prince Dmitrii. However, the principality was not yet safe from attack. In 1382 the new walls, which were still under construction, could not resist a new assault by the Tatars. After a

△ The Kremlin fortress of white stone, which Prince Dmitrii Ivanovich, called Donskoi, had built after the fire of 1365. Pictorial reconstruction by Apolinari Vasnetsov (Moscow, 1922).

three-day siege, Khan Tokhtamish captured Moscow and set it afire. Dmitrii therefore further extended the ring of fortifications in the following years and had 19 towers erected, six of them with gates and barbican towers.

Bitter struggles between the medieval feudal states accompanied Moscow's economic and political ascent at that time. During the early 1470s, the situation came to a head. For fear of the increasing strength of Moscow, the boyars (noblemen) of Novgorod believed they would be safe under the wings of the Lithuanian prince. In 1471, a Muscovite military campaign subdued Novgorod; in 1478, the feudal Novgorod state lost its independence and its entire wealth and fell under the rule of Moscow.

Of even greater historical consequence was the final collapse of Tatar-Mongolian rule in the following decade. The Golden Horde observed the decisive, successful policies of the Muscovite princes with distrust. In 1480, Khan Ahmat set out on a campaign against Moscow, for which he counted on the support of Lithuania. However, when he reached the Ugra, a tributary of the Oka to the left, he came to the realization that his allies had forsaken him for fear of the Muscovites. He thus was forced to retreat with his army to the Nogaya steppe, where he was killed in battle against the Siberian Tatars. This spelled the defeat of the Golden Horde's military might.

Ivan III's Kremlin

After Moscow's annexation of the Grand Principality of Tver in 1485, Ivan III (1440–1505, Grand Prince of Moscow after 1462) had himself declared prince of all Russia. Russia's international reputation grew under his rule. As Karl Marx noted, Europe was more than a little surprised to observe the emergence of a huge state on its eastern borders only shortly after the commencement of Ivan III's reign. Europe had hardly taken notice of the principality of Moscow, caught as it was between the Tatars and the Lithuanians. Not only did Ivan III greatly expand the territory of the principality, but he also overcame Russia's centuries-old cultural isolation from the East and the West. His second marriage, to Zoe-Sophia (in 1472), the niece of the last Byzantine emperor, was brought about by Pope Paul II. In this way, the Grand Prince "inherited" the Byzantine idea of dynasty, which was to lead to tsarism. It was probably Zoe-Sophia's influence that led to Italian builders and architects bringing a breath of the Renaissance to Moscow after about 1475.

Despite its stone walls, the Kremlin fortress built by Dmitrii Donskoi in the 14th century was almost in a state of ruin due to the sieges and fires. Therefore, Ivan III instituted a complete reconstruction program. The mighty enterprise lasted approximately 10 years (from 1485 to 1495) and extended the Kremlin triangle to its present dimensions (circumference 2,235 meters, area 28 hectares). When construction was completed, the residence of a grand prince built according to the rules of city planning and the latest engineering knowledge stood on the former site of a medieval fortress. The basic building material employed was very hard brick. The best builders and artisans from many Russian cities, as well as Italian architects known and respected throughout Europe as military engineers, designed and built the new Kremlin. Ivan III entrusted the Italian engineers Marco Ruffo, Pietro Antonio Solario, Antonio and Marco Friazin, and Alevisio da Carcanno, who were led by Aristotele Fioravante di Ridolfo, with the planning and direction of the project.

The first section erected was the Southern Kremlin wall on the bank of the Moskva River from 1485 to 1489, as the majority of enemy attacks could be expected to come from this direction. For topographical reasons, the height of the wall to the top of the coping varied from five to 19 meters and the thickness of the walls from three and one-half to six and one-half meters. A battlement provided protection for the two-to-four-and-one-half-meter-wide coping.

The placement of the towers required a careful examination of the topography, defense technology, and attack tactics. In 1485, Antonio Friazin constructed the first watchtower (Tainitskaia Tower) and equipped it with a well and a secret opening to the Moskva to ensure a water supply in case of siege. Two years later, a round corner tower designed by

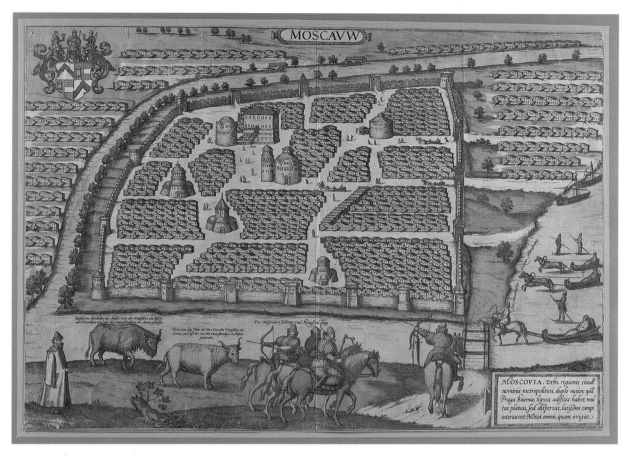

△ Map of Moscow by S. Herberstein, published in Basel in 1556.

Marco Friazin was built near the estate of the boyar Beklemishev, whose name it still bears today. Another corner tower was placed at the point where the Neglinnaia flowed into the Moskva, not far from the estate of the Sviblov boyar family, for whom the tower was then named. Later, this tower was provided with a waterwheel that pumped river water through a lead pipe to the gardens in the upper Kremlin and also gave the tower a new name, Vodovoznaia (Water-Pumping Tower). During those same years, the four watchtowers along the Moskva bank were erected: Blagoveshchenskaia Tower, the First and Second Bezymiannaia (Nameless) Towers, and Peter Tower. That made a total of seven monumental defense towers reaching skyward at the completion of operations on the Kremlin's southern flank.

In 1490–1491, Pietro Antonio Solario completed two especially imposing gate towers: Borovitskaia Tower on the western side of the Kremlin and on the east, Konstantin Yelena Tower, which replaced Timofei Tower. A year later, the same architect erected the Frolovskaia and Nikolskaia Towers. The chronicles report that the latter stood on newly developed terrain and that a wall extended from it down to the Neglinnaia.

A fortified residence which had been built by Italian Renaissance architects commissioned by a grand prince with monarchist tendencies naturally could not be solely comprised of plain, military structures. However, at this point the glorious churches and palaces, to which a special chapter is devoted, will not be discussed. It was thought that the walls and towers should symbolize the concept of a centralist state and represent it through their magnificence. At that time, it was well known how important architectural form and

27

symbols were, and careful attention was paid to which monuments were created to oneself and for the future. Therefore, there were good reasons for putting up the white stone slabs with carved Latin and Old Russian inscriptions over the gate of Frolovskaia Tower that lead to Red Square. They are among the oldest inscriptions in Moscow.

The third corner tower, the Uglovaia-Arsenalnaia, was created in 1492. It was originally called Sobakina Tower, for the boyar family whose estate was located nearby. At the same time, a brick tower was laid between Spasskaia and Nikolskaia Towers. Later, in the 18th century, it was named the Senate Tower, for the former Senate building situated behind it.

The extensive building program started by Ivan III suffered some setbacks. Building activities were interrupted twice when wooden parts and scaffolding on the towers, as well as a temporary wooden wall, were destroyed by fire. When construction resumed in 1492, the most difficult part of the project, on the swampy bank of the Neglinnaia, still lay ahead. Among other things, extensive hydraulic preparatory work was necessary. A deep moat was dug in front of Borovitskaia Tower, where the Neglinnaia flowed quite a distance from the Kremlin walls. Several dams and locks were built on the Neglinnaia itself to divert the accumulated water to the moat.

In 1495, the imposing line of towers on the Neglinnaia flank was completed: Troitskaia, Middle Arsenal, Commandant, Armory, and Facet Towers. The latter is thought to be located on the site of a corner tower built earlier, under Dmitrii Donskoi. The somewhat

△ Ivan III's Kremlin. Pictorial reconstruction by Apolinari Vasnetsov (Moscow, 1922).

▷ Detail from one of the many towers along the red Kremlin wall.

28

smaller Nabatnaia (Alarm) Tower on the east leg of the wall triangle dates from the same time. Of the 20 Kremlin towers, 19 are part of the mighty enclosing wall. Kutafia Tower is the one exception. It was placed forward on the far side of the Neglinnaia moat and connected to Troitskaia Tower by a bridge.

The Kremlin towers were constructed in accordance with the latest rules on military engineering and technology. Not only could the area in front of the Kremlin be swept with artillery fire from the Kremlin, but also the strip of land directly adjacent to the wall. Each tower was an independent citadel and could remain defensible even after neighboring sectors and towers had been captured. The five gate towers were equipped with barbican towers on the outer side, with side galleries, and with stores of cannonballs and were secured by draw-bridges and portcullises. Should the enemy reach one of the barbicans, the portcullises would be dropped, thus trapping the assailants. Although the portcullises and barbicans have not been preserved, today one can still recognize the hewn guide slots for them on Borovitskaia Tower. At the corners of the Kremlin walls, circular towers were built. They made possible a defense from all sides and had wells for drinking water, which guaranteed a certain amount of independence. The well in Arsenal Tower still exists. The corbels of the towers usually had machicolations through which shots could be fired at the enemy at the foot of the bulwark. The merlons were shaped like swallows' tails, a clear indication of their Italian origin. For fire control purposes, cleared areas of land were planned around the fortress and all wooden buildings on a strip of land about 220 meters long were torn down on the far sides of the Neglinnaia and Moskva Rivers. The Tsar's Garden, which existed until the end of the 17th century, arose at this spot.

In 1499, a wing masonry wall was built inside the Kremlin from Borovitskaia Tower to protect the estate of the grand prince from conflagration. This completed the construction of the new wall and Kremlin towers.

Ivan III's Moscow Kremlin was correctly considered an outstanding example of fortress architecture and incorporated the most advanced military engineering knowledge of the time. To the southwest and south, the Neglinnaia and Moskva Rivers provided a natural defense for Borovitskii Hill. On the Red Square side, a 32-meter-wide, approximately two-meter-deep moat connecting the two rivers was dug at the beginning of the 16th century. In 1515, the hydraulic installations were finished. Kutafia Tower and the stone bridge over the Neglinnaia connecting it to Troitskaia Tower also date from this time. The other crossings

▷ The first Nameless Tower, destroyed and rebuilt several times, most recently in 1812–1813.

were protected by drawbridges. The Kremlin remained an island fortress able to withstand all enemy assaults until sometime in the 19th century.

Each of the Kremlin towers has its own unmistakable architectural character, its own purpose, and its own history. In later centuries, superstructures were added to the towers, were decorated, and frequently were renamed. Since the 1780s they have no longer appeared to be gloomy medieval structures but instead the quintessence of cheerfulness. Some of them have been adorned with attractive pointed "tents." Colorful glaze and enamel tiles, gilded eaves, and imaginative weathervanes lend them a picturesque, festive appearance.

Spasskaia Tower, probably the best designed and most majestic of the Kremlin towers, occupies a special position among them. It was, and still is, considered the main entrance to the Kremlin. Its second name, Holy Gate, dates from the Middle Ages and expresses the great respect the people had for it. Grand princes, tsars, and emperors entered the Kremlin through Spasskiia Gate, and foreign ambassadors and their retinues were led to the citadel from this point. On the main church holidays, the highest church dignitaries led parades and processions through this gate to Red Square. Until 1658 the tower was called Frolovskaia, probably after the Frol and Lawr Church nearby, but it was renamed Spasskaia Tower for the icon of the Savior *spas* above its gate.

The Kremlin towers were usually named either for their function (like the Water Tower) or for nearby buildings. Some of the original names have been retained to the present: Borovitskaia, Tainitskaia, Beklemishevskaia, and Nikolskaia Towers have never been called anything else.

Over the course of many centuries, the Kremlin's supplies of food and fodder for horses was brought through Borovitskiia Gate. Linguists attribute this name to the Russian word for forest, *bor,* especially in view of the fact that the Kremlin hill originally was densely wooded. In the 17th century an attempt was made to rename it Redeemer Tower, but the older name prevailed.

Troitskaia Tower (also called Troitskiia Gate) received its name in 1658 from Trinity Monastery located nearby (*troitsa* meaning "trinity"). Before then it had borne the names Kuriatnaia, Snamenskaia, and Bogoyavlenskaia. This gate leads to the palaces of the patriarch and the tsarinas.

▷ Blagoveshchenskaia Tower, built from 1487–1488, as seen from the bank of the Moskva.

St. Nicholas Gate leads to the boyar estates and monasteries in the northeastern part of the Kremlin. Above the gate, on the side facing Red Square, is the icon of its namesake, Nicholas the Miracle Worker.

As of the 17th century Konstantin Yelena Tower, located near Konstantin Yelena Church, no longer served as an entrance. Therefore, the gate was sealed off and the tower used as a prison for quite some time.

Nor did Tainitskaia Tower serve as an entrance for long. Its name probably derives from a secret entrance (*taina* meaning "secret") leading from the Kremlin wall to the banks of the Moskva, which was intended to ensure a supply of water during emergencies. Later, church processions usually left the Kremlin for the Moskva through this gate. After alterations in the 1870s, the superstructure on Tainitskiia Gate was not rebuilt. Although Campioni added it to the tower again in 1862 and cannons were installed on its upper platforms, the superstructure was torn down in 1930 and the gate filled in. The outline of the gate's arch can still be seen on the façade.

Many Kremlin towers were renamed in the 17th century. Frolovskaia became Spasskaia Tower; Kuriatnaia became Troitskaia Tower; Sviblov became the Water Tower; and Timofei, the Konstantin Yelena Tower. From that period also date names such as Blagoveshchenskaia Tower, for the Church of the Annunciation nearby; Kolymazhnaia (Carriage) Tower, for the Office of Coaches in the vicinity; Konyushennaia (Stable) Tower, for the Office of Stables; and Nabat (Alarm) Tower, for the alarm bell hung there. The renaming of the Kremlin towers continued in the following centuries. For example, Peter Tower received its name in the 18th century (because the Church of St. Peter was erected in its vicinity), as did the Senate Tower (for the Senate Building). After the Armory was built, two more towers were renamed: Sobakin Tower was thereafter known as the Corner Arsenal Tower, and the Facet Tower became the Middle Arsenal Tower.

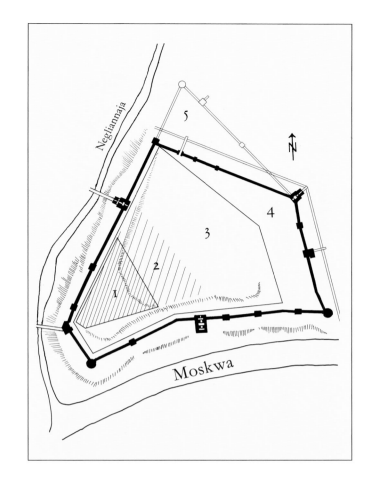

▷ Expansion of the Moscow Kremlin from the 12th to the 16th century: 1. Mid-12th-century (Iurii Dolgorukii); 2. Second half of the 12th century; 3. First half of the 14th century (Ivan Kalita); 4. 1365–1370 (Whitestone Moscow); 5. End of the 15th century (Ivan III) and present boundaries.

▽ Inner side of the Kremlin wall; Senate and Nikolskaia Towers.

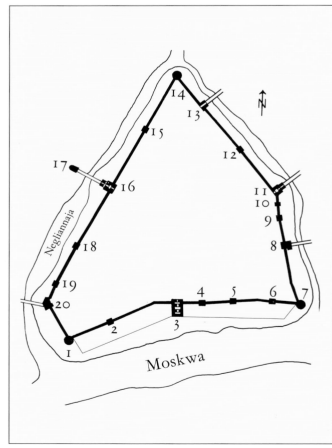

△ Wall along the Moskva and part of the ring of towers. In the foreground, the first Nameless Tower.

◁ The present towers around the Moscow Kremlin: 1. Water-Pumping Tower (1488, restored 1817–1819); 2. Blagoveshchenskaia Tower (1487–1488); 3. Tainitskaia Tower (1485, rebuilt 1771–1773); 4. First Nameless Tower (1783, blown up 1812 and subsequently rebuilt); 5. Second Nameless Tower (superstructure added in 1680); 6. Peter Tower (restored 1812); 7. Beklemishev Tower (1487); 8. Konstantin Yelena Tower (1490); 9. Alarm Tower (1495); 10. Tsar Tower (1680); 11. Spasskaia Tower (1491); 12. Senate Tower (1491, superstructure added 1680); 13. Nikolskaia Tower (1491, superstructure added 1816); 14. Corner Arsenal Tower (1492, rebuilt 1812); 15. Middle Arsenal Tower (1495); 16. Troitskaia Tower (1495, superstructure added 1685, new clock 1686); 17. Kutafia Tower (1495, superstructure added 1685, altered 1867; 18. Commandant Tower (1495); 19. Armory Tower (1495); 20. Borovitskaia Tower (1490).

▷ View of Spasskaia Tower from Red Square.

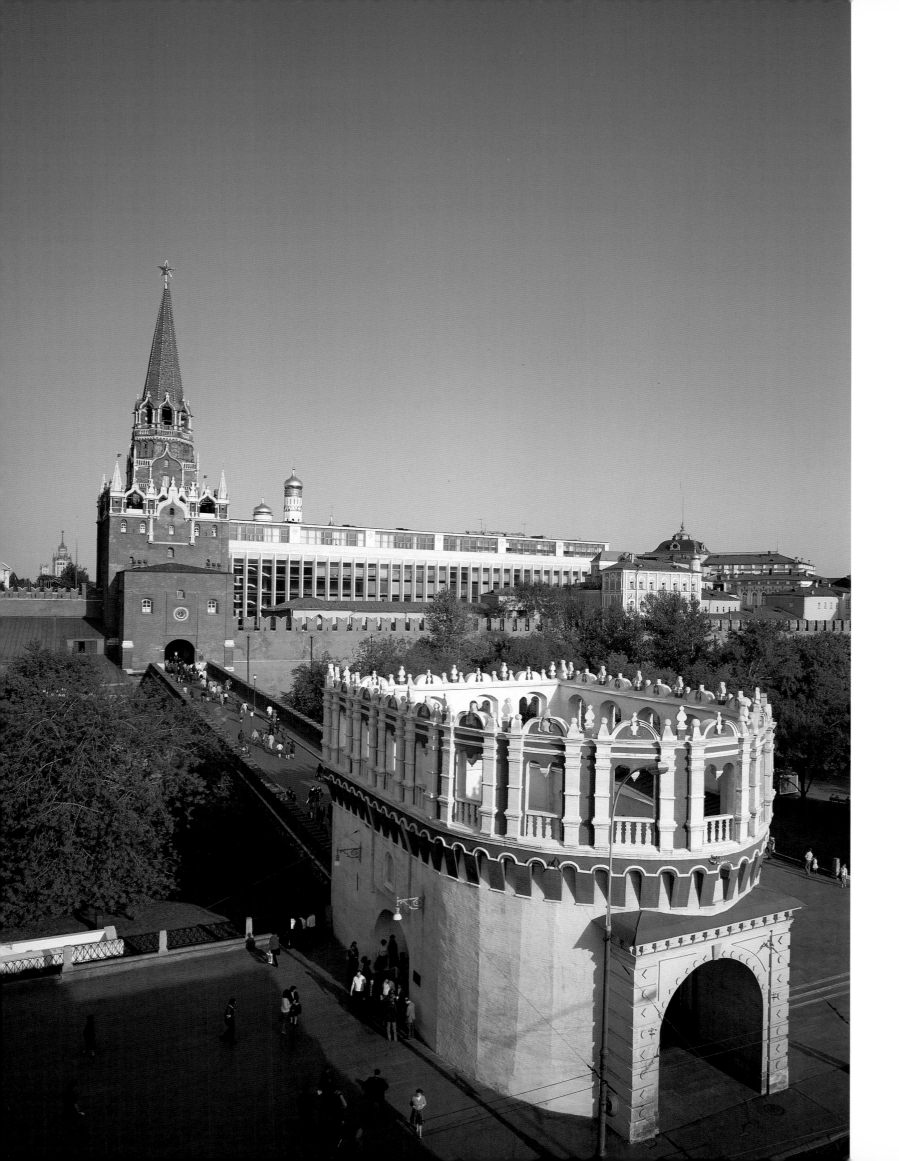

◁ ◁ Kutafia Tower, which served as a barbican, with Troitskaia Tower in the background.

◁ Nikolskaia Tower, decorated in Neo-Gothic style.

▽ View from Tsar Tower towards the Cathedral of St. Basil the Blessed on Red Square.

Page 40: Kremlin walls, Spasskaia and Tsar Towers. In the foreground, the Place of the Brow, the site of public executions.

Page 41: Section of the wall on the Moskva River. In the background, the domes of the ecclesiastical buildings on Cathedral Square.

The Center of the Tsarist Realm

After Ivan III's death, his son Vasilii III ruled from 1505 to 1533. He completed a number of buildings which his father had begun. Above all, the cathedrals and palaces were adorned with murals and products of artisanship, an undertaking which kept the various manufactures and workshops busy for years. The Russian state acquired definite centralistic traits during Vasilii III's regime. His son Ivan IV, called Grozny (the Severe or, because of his cruelty, the Terrible), was merely three years old when Vasilii died. After spending an unhappy youth filled with intrigues and power struggles, he assumed the regency in 1547 and on January 16 had himself crowned Tsar and Autocrat of All Russia by Metropolitan Makarii in the Cathedral of the Assumption. The first tsar initiated promising reforms; however, more and more of them failed due to his autocratic arbitrariness, which ended in a pathological despotism that severely damaged the state and laid waste to entire regions. Within the Kremlin walls, Ivan Grozny continued the building program; above all else, he expanded the tsar's residence at the expense of boyars' estates, had alterations made to the Tsar's Palace, and had several administration and farm buildings erected.

On the whole, the Kremlin underwent a stormy 16th century. Moscow was repeatedly attacked by the Tatars and struck by fires. The army of the Khan of the Crimea, Mohammed Girai, unexpectedly advanced almost to the Kremlin walls in the summer of 1521, but could not take the fortress and retreated in late summer just as suddenly as it had come. A brick wall was erected around the outlying settlements, especially around Kitai Gorod, the City of the Chinese, from 1533 to 1583, so that the two fortresses formed a defensible unit in Moscow's center. In 1547, a fire in the city caused widespread damage in the Kremlin. The gunpowder stored in secret depots of three towers exploded, resulting in much destruction, especially on the southern part of the ring wall. In 1571, the Khan of the Crimea, Deflet-Girai, attempted retaliation for the defeat of the Tatars in Kazan and Astrakhan. He marched to the gates of Moscow with a mighty army supposedly numbering about 100,000. The suburbs were once again set on fire and many lives lost, yet the Kremlin also withstood this attack. After Deflet-Girai's retreat, the suburbs were rebuilt and the fortifications expanded. At the place where Boulevard Ring now extends through the city, a six-meter-high bulwark was erected. Fifteen years later, a third ring of defense was added. Feodor Kony, who had won distinction for the wall around the fortress in Smolensk, directed its construction. Thus arose the "White City" toward the end of the 16th century. The monasteries in and around Moscow also gained in size, political influence, and military importance during this period, among them the Simonov and Danilov Monasteries and the New Monastery of Our Savior, all of which are situated within the present city boundaries.

Under Khan Kazi-Girai, the Tatars again endeavored to attack Moscow in 1591, but this last Tatar attempt at invasion also failed. Subsequently, however, a palisade was hurriedly set up around all of Moscow in such a short time that the wooden wall was later commonly called *Skorodom* (Rapid Building). Thus, near the end of the turbulent 16th century, four walls enclosed Moscow, including about 120 towers and several fortified monasteries, among them the New Monastery of the Holy Virgin. Another monastery-fortress was located on the main square of the city directly in front of the Spasskaia Gate: the Vasilii Blazhenny Cathedral (built 1554–1560). It was connected to the Kremlin by an underground passage and was supposed to ward off the first wave of enemy attacks. In 1600, the Belfry of Ivan the Great was erected on Cathedral Square in the Kremlin. Designed as a watchtower, it afforded a view of all of Moscow.

No less complicated and eventful was the 17th century, which went down in history as "the time of troubles." Bitter fighting took place for the tsar's throne following the death of Ivan the Terrible in 1584. On May 15, 1591, Dmitrii, Ivan's youngest son, died under circumstances never fully clarified. The throne at that time belonged to his older brother Feodor, who lacked willpower, was weak-minded, and was also not in very good health. His brother-in-law, Boris Godunov, officially the regent for the underaged tsar, was the de facto ruler. Since Feodor had left no heir to the throne, the death of the rightful successor, Dmitrii, quite clearly paved Godunov's path to the throne. According to the official report, Prince (Tsarevich) Dmitrii, who had been brought to Uglich by his supporters to shield him from Boris Godunov, fell onto a knife during an epileptic attack and died immediately. However, the people did not believe this story and suspected Godunov of being behind Dmitrii's death. Significantly, Boris Godunov was the only tsar whose tomb was not accorded a place in the Kremlin, whereas the mortal remains of Dmitrii were brought to Moscow after Godunov's death and re-interred with all the honors due a tsar.

In 1598 Feodor, the last remaining son of Ivan IV, died. A new tsar had to be elected. Whether it was the shadow of the murdered prince, the cruel laws of serfdom, or the terrible famine, dissatisfaction, rebellion, and unrest continued without end. Feuding between the boyars escalated. Several pretenders to the throne saw a chance for themselves amidst the utter confusion. In mid-1602, a man at the court of the Polish ruler claimed to be the tsar's son Dmitrii and to have miraculously escaped the attempt on his life. Toward the end of 1604, he started off on a campaign against Russia with an army of mercenaries. As the fighting neared its climax in 1605, Boris Godunov died and his 16-year-old son ascended to the Russian throne. A part of the boyar opposition subsequently joined the ranks of the "False

Dmitrii." He marched to Moscow, set fire to the suburbs, and entered the Kremlin by cunning and deceit. On July 21, 1605, he had himself crowned tsar in the Cathedral of the Assumption. When he married Maryna, the daughter of the Polish magnate J. Mniztsech, on May 8 of the following year, a storm of indignation broke out among the Muscovite boyars. On May 17, the ringing of the Kremlin Alarm Bell interrupted the boisterous wedding festivities. Conspirators from the boyar camp opposed to Poland killed the usurper to the throne and threw his corpse on the Place of the Brow, where public executions were carried out on Red Square. They then proceeded to appoint Vasilii Shuiskii, a man from their own ranks, to the throne.

However, this did not put an end to the unrest. A peasants' revolt against feudalism led by Ivan Bolotnikov had by then taken hold of the entire country, and the peasants were marching on Moscow. The city barely survived a five-week siege. Not until the spring of 1607 did the boyars succeed in suppressing the uprising begun the previous year and capturing Bolotnikov, who was blinded and drowned in Kargopol in 1608. Yet in the summer of 1607, another pretender had already taken advantage of the precarious domestic political situation. False Dmitrii II was able to unite the peasants and Kossacks scattered by the defeat of Bolotnikov to form a strong army within a short time. The Russian people's unbroken belief in a good and just tsar eased this adventurer's way to the walls and gates of Moscow. Although he was unable to take the capital by storm, the treachery of frightened boyars opened the gates for him. Once again, the usurper died at the hands of a murderer. False Dmitrii II was slain by a Tatar prince while hunting on December 11, 1610.

Devastated and destroyed several times, Moscow always succeeded in regaining its position in the center of politics. In January 1613, a class parliament was convened in the city to elect a tsar. Because the villeins were not admitted to the parliament, the big landowners were the sole members. The election office turned down all foreign aspirants to the throne outright and chose 16-year-old Michail Romanov, the scion of one of the most respected dynasties in Russia, as the new tsar in the Cathedral of the Assumption on February 21. The first years of his reign were stormy. Danger threatened from the Polish realm, which wanted to set its own Prince Vladislav on the Russian throne at all costs. In the north, Sweden did not leave Russia in peace. Tatars from the Crimea regularly ravaged the southern border regions. In many places, the peasants rebelled against the big landowners and local rulers. The situation did not quiet down until a peace treaty for fourteen and one-half years was signed between the Polish empire and Russia on December 1, 1618, after an unsuccessful Polish attempt to conquer Moscow.

44

△ The Sigismund map of Moscow, drawn up in 1610.

Moscow took advantage of the peaceful period that ensued. New buildings and alterations in the Kremlin and adjoining areas changed the city's appearance considerably. Several palaces, churches, and cathedrals, as well as buildings for various public offices, were erected. Somewhat later, in the second half of the 17th century, stone "tents" were added to many of the Kremlin towers and the fortifications were carefully improved (by reinforcing the socle, restoring the merlons, and renovating entire sections of the wall). In 1618, the same year the peace treaty was signed, the small Tsar Tower was built south of Spasskaia Tower. A wooden tower is purported to have stood on this site previously, from which it is said that Ivan the Terrible watched the hustle and bustle and − with particular pleasure − the executions on Red Square. The new Tsar Tower had graceful columns, an attractive tent roof and an imaginative weather vane. It also housed the Kremlin's two alarm bells. Later, only one bell remained in the Kremlin (in Nabatnaia, the Alarm Tower). An especially fascinating episode is connected with it: when the Plague Uprising broke out in 1771, the rebels rang the bell. Government troops crushed the people's rage. Empress Catherine II ordered a search for the man who had rung the alarm bell, but since the search was unsuccessful, imperial punishment was meted out to the bell itself: its tongue was torn out. The mute bell hung for over 30 years in the tower until it was taken down in 1803 and set up in the Arsenal. Later, it was accorded a more honorable spot in the Armory, where one can see it today. The inscription on the bell reads, "On the 30th day of June in the year 1714, this alarm bell was cast from an old alarm bell for the Kremlin city and Spasskaia Tower. It weighs 150 pud. This bell was cast by Master Ivan Motorin" – from whose workshop the huge Tsar Kolokol Bell also comes.

In 1625, a tent-shaped superstructure with several bells and a clock was added on to Spasskaia Tower. A fire destroyed these additions in 1654, but they were quickly rebuilt. At about the same time, a stone arched bridge, 10 meters wide and 42 meters long, was erected over the moat. It soon became a favorite spot in Moscow and attracted all sorts of tradesmen. One could purchase rare books, prints, and various and sundry antiques and products of craftsmanship on this bridge until into the 19th century. Spasskaia Tower has ten stories; three are taken up by the clockwork of the Kremlin chimes, which has a remarkable history. The Moscow Kremlin received its first "clock" in 1404. At that time, a monk named Lazarus set up a "time machine" on Cathedral Square near the Cathedral of the Annunciation. News of this fantastic technical wonder spread throughout Europe. A real tower clock probably told the time and struck the hours for the Kremlin soon after Spasskaia Tower was constructed (in 1491, then called Frolovskaia Tower). In the 16th century, clocks were also installed in Troitskaia and Tainitskaia Towers. The chronicles' report about the clockwork built in the 17th century commands a special interest. Christopher Holloway, an English clockmaker in service to Russia, received the commission for the clock on Spasskaia Tower in 1621. Russian artisans assisted him: Shdan and his son, who were responsible for the forging, and Kirill Samoilov, who did the decorative casting. Several features of this clock strike us as unusual today: the clockface was divided into 17 sections instead of 12 and revolved, while a "sunbeam" from above served as an immovable hand. Despite – or perhaps due to – its strange construction, the Holloway clock did not function for very long. Therefore, Tsar Peter I had the machinery for a new clock made in Amsterdam in 1704 and brought to Moscow on 30 carts, a trip that lasted from 1706 to 1709. Nikofor Jakolev and his journeymen installed the huge apparatus in Spasskaia Tower, but it also soon stopped running, and it broke down completely after the dramatic city fire in 1737. A hundred years later, the clockwork that still functions today was set up in the tower

▷ The Water-Pumping Tower, built in 1488, blown up in 1812, rebuilt from 1817to 1819. A striking, slender round tower on the southwest corner of the Kremlin grounds.

46

during the great renovation of the Kremlin. K. Ton had the upper chambers of the tower altered for this clock. N. and P. Butenop put the mighty machinery together in 1851–1852. The cylinder for the chimes was programmed with the melodies to "Kol Slaven" and "The March of the Preobrazhenskii Regiment." The mechanism, comprised of three blocks, is now located on the seventh, eighth, and ninth floors. The four clockfaces each measure 6.12 meters in diameter; the numbers are 72 centimeters high; and the hour hand is 1.97 and the minute hand, 3.28 meters long. Three weights between 160 and 224 kilograms keep the clockwork in motion while a pendulum weighing 32 kilograms ensures that the clock runs accurately. A hammer connected to the clockwork strikes the quarter hours. The numerous bells, lavishly adorned with inscriptions and ornaments, date from the 17th and 18th centuries. One of the inscriptions states that this particular bell was created especially for the Spasskaia clock: "This bell on Spasskaia Tower strikes every quarter-hour and was cast on the 27th day of May in 1769, with a weight of 21 pud [336 kilograms] by Semyon Mossuchin."

The Office of Armaments, responsible for the Kremlin's military equipment, kept a faithful record of the renovation of the Kremlin fortifications in the 1680s. According to their records, the Russian artisans Yeremei Pyatov and Yakov Dikov and Prince Baryatinki's villeins did a great amount of work on the structures. Although cannons were still set up in the Kremlin, gunpowder still stored in the cellars, and the "streltsy" (guards) kept watch on the walls, the bulwarks of the Kremlin began to lose their function as defense structures and their sinister appearance towards the end of the century. The Kremlin's fortress character visibly gave way to the tsar's residence. Even Ivan III had started to blow a breath of the Renaissance into the architecture of the Kremlin and the complex as a whole. After two centuries of grand princes' and tsars' households and constant renovations, the Kremlin had become an extended, complex seat of the court by around 1700.

At the same time as the Kremlin, Moscow had gradually taken on a new shape. A noisy, turbulent activitiy unfolded in the aspiring capital. Economically, socially, and culturally, bitter struggles arose between the social classes. Everyone strove to become a part of the goings-on, lured by the promise of bread and a comfortable life: large landowners, nouveau riche merchants, and the horde of small tradesmen, artisans, and peasants looking for ways to earn money. The available space no longer sufficed even for the estates of the princes and the most prominent boyars. Courtiers of all ranks, industrious government employees, and priests and popes of the Russian Church all wanted to move into the White City – or better yet, the Kremlin proper – at all costs, thus pushing the less influential tradesmen and

△ Red Square in the second half of the 17th century. In the background, St. Basil's Cathedral; to its right, Spasskaia Tower. Pictorial reconstruction by Apolinari Vasnetsov (Moscow, around 1920).

artisans into the outlying areas. Following a medieval tradition, the members of a guild were accustomed to living near each other, so that entire settlements of artisans and tradesmen gradually formed; historians estimate that over 140 arose in the 17th century alone, among them the Guards' Village, Potters' Village, and Smiths' Village.

Populous Moscow contained a colorful mixture of nationalities around 1700. Some ethnic groups, such as the Ukrainians, the Byelorussians, the Armenians, and the Georgians, founded their own settlements. The influx of foreigners also grew stronger; they came from all over Europe and served in Moscow as officers, doctors, pharmacists, or artisans. The word *nemzy (nem* meaning "mute") originated with them and applied to all people who could not speak Russian (not until later did the word come to mean "German"). The foreigners settled chiefly in Nemetskaii Soboda, Foreigners Village, on the Yauza.

The rapidly expanding Moscow metropolis also witnessed fierce social class struggles between the proletariat, clerks, and civil servants on the one hand and the despised boyars, unscrupulous magnates, and profit-hungry merchants on the other. In addition, epidemics, fires, and natural disasters shaped the rather dreary daily life in this large, pre-modern city.

△ Clockface on Spasskaia Tower.

▽ View of the side of the Kremlin facing the river, during the 17th and 18th centuries. Pictorial reconstruction by Apolinari Vasnetsov (Moscow, 1922).

The Glory and Distress of the Moscow Kremlin in the 18th and 19th Centuries

On the threshold of the 18th century, a new calendar was introduced in Russia: in the future, the year would not begin on September 1, but rather on January 1. The reformation of the calendar is only one of the numerous innovations that the great reformer of Russia, Peter I (1672–1725, tsar as of 1682), thought necessary. In the meantime, the international situation deteriorated culminating in a war against Sweden, the Great Northern War (1700–1721).

Peter I found no pleasure in Moscow, with its arrogant and, in part, dull boyars and eternally mutinous *streltsy* (citizens and merchants who fulfilled hereditary military service). The enlightened ruler felt much better far away from the Kremlin, in such places as Lefortovo (a part of Germantown) or the settlement of the Preobrazhenskii Regiment. It was neither a coincidence nor a whim, therefore, that led to his having a new capital built in St. Petersburg, for Moscow was the stronghold of the boyars, who clung to their traditions and privileges.

The Russian troops suffered a devastating defeat in the Great Northern War near Narva in November 1700. Peter I reacted by reforming the army, which led to its first victory only two years later. Supposedly, the first salute to a military victory was fired in the Kremlin at that time. From 1707 to 1709, the army of Charles XII of Sweden penetrated ever deeper into Russia. The Kremlin prepared its defenses feverishly for the coming battle: embankments were thrown up, moats dug, and bulwarks and other fortifications added. Prince Aleksei, who observed the preparations at close range, wrote his father: "In front of the Borovitskaia Tower, [the ground] is being dug out down to the foundations and directly afterward, construction of the bulwark will be commenced. The embrasures in the Kremlin towers are being widened so that the cannon can fire through them." Over 3,000 *streltsy* and officers and 245 artillerymen manning almost 1,000 cannons were to defend the Kremlin against the Swedish troops. When the Battle of Poltava (June 27–July 8, 1709) turned the tides of the war, Moscow celebrated with matchless enthusiasm for several days. Peter I himself gave a banquet in the Chamber of Facets. On the whole, it is clear that Peter I did not neglect Moscow, even though he was chiefly interested in the new capital on the Neva River. After the catastrophic fire of 1701, he gave orders that only stone structures were to be built within the Kremlin, China Village, and the White City. When St. Petersburg became the official capital in 1713 and the government of the Russian empire moved to the new city, Moscow remained the "capital of the throne" (place of coronation) and "secondary capital." As the emperor of all Russia, Peter I also celebrated the peace of Nystadt

(1721), which ended the Great Northern War, in the Kremlin. This started the tradition in Moscow of celebrating the events most important for Russia's fate.

During the 18th century, Moscow further strengthened its position as the hub of manufacturing and trade and also developed into a center of higher education. It is therefore not surprising that the first geodetic map of Moscow was drawn up at that time (by Ivan Michurin in 1739), providing a realistic representation of the topography and development plan. As always, the nobility felt at home there. Despite these factors, Moscow was apparently a rather vacant and sleepy place, according to records from that period. Obvious signs of neglect soon appeared. In addition, a widespread fire in the city charred the wooden parts of the fortifications and damaged the gate towers' bridges. The bells in Spasskaia Tower fell and crashed through the floors below.

During the lifetime of Catherine II (1729 – 1796, Empress as of 1762), many ideas were put forth for changing Moscow. Of particular interest for Kremlin history is the design for a huge palace drawn by Vassili Ivanovich Bazhenov, the outstanding Russian architect of the time. A pompous façade was planned for the grandiose building, which was intended to face the Moskva River and to unite the older Kremlin buildings in a new ensemble. Preparatory work was initiated on Tainitskaia and the Second Nameless Towers and on the adjoining sections of the wall. In 1773, the cornerstone was ceremoniously laid for the palace. However, it then became apparent that the state treasury was empty; the extravagant life at court and the war had left their marks. Thus, the gigantic construction project was stopped – forever, as it turned out. Bazhenov's ingenious design was realized only on paper. However, a model of the palace was created according to his design and is on display in the branch of the A. Shtchusev Museum of Russian Architecture located in Donskoy Monastery. The preparatory work already carried out on the fortifications was undone after the premature end of the project. Despite occasional construction work on the walls and residences, the Kremlin appeared desolate and abandoned toward the end of the 18th century.

The beginning of the 19th century found Moscow in a new upswing. In anticipation of Alexander I's coronation as tsar of Russia, the order of the day was "Order and Cleanliness." Hurriedly, the moats were filled in, the bulwarks from the time of Peter I were leveled, and the decaying Coat of Arms Tower and other buildings on the estate of the grand prince were torn down. In the following year, renovation of several towers and the wall was begun. First

Pages 54–55: View of Moscow from the balcony of the Imperial Palace. 1799 lithograph by Gerard Delabarth, printed in 1810.

▷ Section of the map drawn up under the direction of Ivan Michurin in 1739. The map clearly shows the expansion of the core of the settlement (the Kremlin) into the swelling metropolis.

52

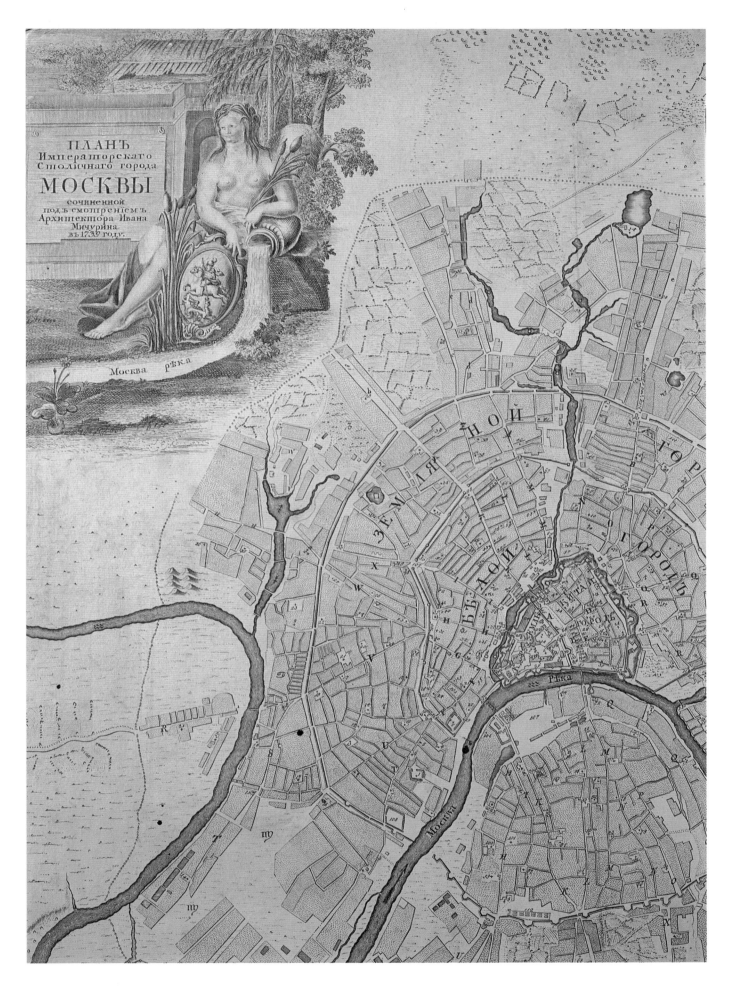

ПЛАНЪ
Императорскаго
Столичнаго города
МОСКВЫ
сочиненной
подъ смотрѣніемъ
Архитектора Ивана
Мичурина
въ 1739 году.

Москва рѣка

53

Vue de la Ville de Moscou prise de la gauche du Balcon du Palais Imperial

Cette vue & la précédente sont les plus belles de la Collection. On les doit à l'empressement que Sa Majesté Paul Premier fit paroître de les avoir en peinture. On y découvre une partie de l'enceinte du Kremlin, tout ce qui est de la ville sous ce point de vue & tout ce qui s'étend au delà.

Entrepris aux fraix de Jean Walser, Négociant de la première Classe à Moscou publié en 1799 avec Privilège de Sa Majesté Impériale Paul Premier Empereur

in line was the flank facing Red Square. A tent roof was added to Nikolskaia Tower, although in Gothic style, unlike the others. The Water-Pumping Tower proved to be in a state of ruin and had to be torn down to its foundation and completely rebuilt. Weathering had advanced to such a dangerous degree on many sections of the wall and in the towers that the façades and merlons were renovated and partly covered with stone slabs. This renovation for "order and cleanliness" cost the magnificent sum of 110,000 rubles.

Then came 1812. Napoleon I's great army defeated all its opponents on the battlefields of Western Europe, and a victory over Russia was all that remained to seal the supremacy of France. Napoleon I's main goal was to defeat Moscow. For the Russians, Moscow symbolized their entire mother country in this war. Every available force was called upon to defend the former capital: new units and formations as well as civilians for home reserves were recruited; foodstuffs, clothing, and horse fodder were stockpiled for emergencies.

In the meantime, Napoleon's troops swept on toward their goal. On August 26 (September 7, according to the new calendar), the Battle of Borodino (west of Moscow) was fought, which decisively influenced the further course of the war and proved to be one of the most astonishing battles, with some of the heaviest losses, in the history of warfare. Despite the numerical superiority of the French army, the Russian troops succeeded in inflicting casualties on their opponent from which the "Grand Army" would never recover. The awareness that they were defending the very heart of Russia in fighting for Moscow lent the Russian soldiers strength and courage. In the aftermath of the battle, when neither opponent was able to decide who had won and who had lost, M. Kutusov, the Russian commander, decided to continue the retreat after a council of war held in Moscow Fili on September 1. The troops and inhabitants abandoned Moscow without a battle.

On September 2, Napoleon expected a delegation from Moscow to kneel before him and present him the keys to the city. But instead, an empty, silent city awaited him. Five days later, the French troops entered the Kremlin. Suddenly, a raging fire broke out in Moscow; historians have been unable to agree on its cause up to the present. The flames spread to other quarters. The French emperor and his retinue watched from the Kremlin while all attempts to quench the blaze failed. The fire swept through Moscow for six full days. A sad sight met Napoleon's eyes: he could see nothing but a sea of flames that seemed to forecast his downfall. ... Napoleon moved from the Kremlin to Peter Palace in one of the Moscow suburbs.

The city lay in smoking ruins: according to official records, the fire destroyed 7,632 of Moscow's 9,151 buildings. Although Napoleon's troops had successfully entered Moscow, on the eve of winter they had neither quarters nor provisions, with no hopes for a truce. The morale of the "Grand Army" sank from day to day, as famine and looting increasingly paralyzed the discipline and standards of the troops. The inhabitants who had remained in the city took up the fight against the invaders. In the space of only one month, Napoleon lost 30,000 soldiers and officers in Moscow before the army started their headlong retreat on October 7. Barbaric is the only word to describe Napoleon's revenge: he ordered the Kremlin blown to pieces. On October 11, the sky above Moscow was rent by terrific explosions. Many sections of the Kremlin wall collapsed and many towers and palaces suffered severe damage. The hardest hit were the Water-Pumping Tower, the First Nameless Tower, Peter Tower, St. Nicholas Tower, The Corner Arsenal Tower, and the Arsenal building. On Cathedral Square, the Philaret building and its small bell tower caved in. The only edifice that remained standing was the Belfry of Ivan the Great, the highest structure in the Kremlin and an historical monument of great symbolic significance.

Marshall Mortier was unable to execute completely his emperor's order to blow up the Kremlin: several Muscovites slipped into the Kremlin at the last minute and extinguished the fuses to powder mines underneath Spasskaia Tower, numerous cathedrals, and sections of the wall, thus preventing the destruction of many priceless architectural monuments. The vanguard of the regular army, the civilian reserves of Moscow, and the Central Russian peasants participated in the flood of merciless Russian retaliatory strikes that followed. The French path of retreat through the rich southern regions was cut off, thus forcing the conquerors to flee back through the same cities and villages they had already plundered wholesale during their advance.

Russia's ravaged and despoiled former capitol was a shocking sight and called for urgent measures of reconstruction. Among others, a building committee was founded to which leading Russian architects belonged. O. Bove rebuilt the Water Tower, the Middle Arsenal Tower, Peter Tower, and Nikolskaia Tower under the direction of the committee. Demian Ivanovich Giliardi reconstructed the small annex on the Belfry of Ivan the Great. The Corner Arsenal Tower, Borovitskaia Tower, and the northern part of the Arsenal were also renovated. The lack of old drawings and the rather hectic pace of reconstruction became painfully apparent, and they led to some architectural alterations that are regrettable when considered from a modern perspective. The bulwarks and moats from the period of Peter I were thought to be superfluous. Numerous small shops along the Kremlin wall were removed to quarters somewhat farther away. The Neglinnaia disappeared into a large pipe. In 1821, Aleksandrovskii Park was laid out in front of the Kremlin wall and could be reached from Troitskii Bridge by way of gently sloping paths. An amusement grotto arose at the foot of the Middle Arsenal Tower. The towers and walls were whitewashed and the tents of the most important towers painted green. The inner chambers of several towers and the wooden gate in Blagoveshchenskaia Tower were renovated, whereas old Portomoiny (Underwear) Gate was sealed off. This gate was named for the palace servants, who always used it as a passageway to the Moskva River when they wanted to do their washing.

After reconstruction, Moscow presented the picture of a large spacious city in which a modern structure was becoming increasingly evident through broad boulevards, ring roads, and grid-pattern neighborhoods. Yet almost 90 percent of its buildings were made of wood up to the end of the 19th century. Formerly a city of the nobility, Moscow had become the domain of manufacturers and merchants. Its industrial output rose considerably. The city ranked at the top of the field of light industry, was a central market for agriculture, and after 1851 formed the main junction of the Russian railway network. Later, it was also the center of the main line of communication, the telegraph. The number of inhabitants grew from 317,800 in 1858 to one million in 1897. However, the city's social inequality contrasted sharply with its well-ordered construction and periodically led to tension and revolts.

The Kremlin experienced a new surge of building activity in the mid-19th century after Tsar Nicholas I, who still resided in St. Petersburg, commissioned the architect Konstantin Andreyevich Ton with a project for a gigantic palace. The renovations on the fortifications were carried out during approximately the same period as the work on the Grand Kremlin Palace, which lasted 11 years; the old structures were restored as closely as possible to their original forms. During this period of the emergence of historicism, this of course led to radical alterations on some buildings. Three leading Russian architects, F. Richter, N. Shokhin, and P. Gerassimov, were among those involved.

▷ △ Military parade in the Kremlin. 1841, oil painting by G. Chernetsov.

▷ View of the Armory façade, which dates from the 19th century.

The Kremlin after the October Revolution of 1917

The 1917 October Revolution marked a turning point in the history of the Moscow Kremlin. The young Soviet Republic, led by Vladimir Lenin, vigorously advocated the preservation of cultural treasures. One of the first appeals made by the Executive Committee of Soviets in Petrograd in November 1917 states: "Citizens! The old rulers of the country are gone. A gigantic inheritance has been left behind which now belongs to the entire people. Citizens! Protect this inheritance, protect paintings, sculptures and buildings; they are an expression of your and your ancestors' intellectual prowess. ... Citizens! Protect monuments, buildings, objects and documents from former times. All of these are your history and your pride. Remember that this is the basis upon which our new art shall flourish!"

As early as December 1917, P. Malinovski, the Commissar of the Office of Palaces in the Kremlin, submitted studies on the reconstruction and renovation of the damaged Kremlin buildings and facilities to the government and urged that a photographic inventory of all monuments damaged during the confusion of the Revolution be taken immediately. On January 5, 1918, an ordinance appeared signed by A. Lunatsharski, the People's Commissar of Education and Culture, decreeing among other things: "All buildings and structures, as well as art and historic monuments, are considered to be the property of the Republic, valid immediately, regardless of what institution or organization, including churches, cathedrals and monasteries, owns or uses them at present."

In March 1918, the Soviet government moved to Moscow. The government resolutions made in those years clearly show that the Soviet of People's Commissars repeatedly dealt with questions of the preservation and restoration of the Moscow Kremlin during their meetings in 1918 and 1919. A committee of experts, the "Commission for the Preservation of Monuments of Art and the Past in the Moscow Soviet," assisted the government from November 1917 to August 1918. On October 5, during a very difficult period, the Soviet of People's Commissars passed the decree "On Listing, Surveying and Preserving the Monuments of Art and the Past in the Possession of Private Citizens, Companies and Organizations." The decree declared privately owned historical monuments and works of art to be public property and placed them under the protection of the state. As a result, numerous groups of researchers comprised of experts and lay persons worked extremely hard to save thousands upon thousands of Russian and international artworks from ruin, theft, capital drain, and smuggling.

During the same period, a department of museums and the preservation of art and cultural monuments was formed at the People's Commissariat (Ministry) of Education. The aforementioned committee of experts was integrated into this department in 1918 and

△ Lenin reading *Pravda* at his desk. Photograph taken on October 16, 1918.

moved into two rooms in the former Noblemen's Corps in the Kremlin. It thus bore the name Kremlin Commission. Its duties included the prevention of the smuggling of art treasures into foreign countries, and for this purpose it had its own troops. They were picketed in front of the entrance to the office: sailors in uniform on trucks with machine-gun ammunition belts across their chests.

It is not surprising that the committee operated out of the Kremlin. During World War I countless paintings, sculptures, products of applied arts and crafts, and objects of historical value were brought to the Kremlin. Some of them came from West Russia, although most of them had been confiscated from the tsar's estate in Beloveshkaia pustsha or had been collected for their protection. The next task was the registration and preservation of the treasures accumulated in the Kremlin. The commission immediately started taking inventory of them and also of the Armory with all its exhibits, the Patriarchal Sacristy, and the Grand Kremlin Palace. The loyal assistance of former imperial civil servants proved invaluable. For example, Vladimir Konstaninovich Trutovki, the former Head Curator of the Armory and a known art expert, and Archimandit Arssenius, former treasurer of the Patriarchal Sacristy and a leading authority on Old Russian art, put their experience at the disposal of the new republic.

The Soviet government set aside 450,000 rubles for the inventory and the Kremlin renovation as early as November 1917. Vladimir I. Lenin's instructions of May 17, 1918, to the commandant of the Kremlin, P. Malkov, indicate how resolutely he supported the restoration of this national monument: "To the Commandant of the Kremlin. Request that Vladimir Gate be restored immediately. P. Malinovski should commission one of the architects with estimating the costs and supervising the work. Chairman of the Soviet of People's Commissars. V. Uljanov (Lenin)." Word had spread that Lenin followed up his instructions with meticulous inspections. Therefore, the Kremlin commandant sent this report only two days later: "To the Chairman of the Soviet of People's Commissars, Comrade Lenin. I herewith report that the necessary measures for the immediate restoration of Vladimir Gate in Nikolskaia Tower have been initiated by me in accordance with your directive, Nr. 2722 of May 17, and that work will commence on May 22 with the highest priority. Commandant of the Kremlin Malkov."

Thus began the first restoration of the Kremlin based on scientific knowledge. Beklemishev and Spasskaia Towers succeeded Nikolskaia Tower. Lenin kept a close watch on the restoration activities. During a walk around the Kremlin, he noticed that the chimes on Spasskaia Tower, the "Chief National Clock," were not functioning. In fact, the clockwork had suffered damage during the fighting in October 1917. In a private talk, Lenin persuaded Nicholai Vassilyevich Berens, one of the old clockmakers, to repair the clock. At the same time, Mikhail Mikhailovich Cheremnykh programmed the cylinder with a new melody. In August 1918 the bells once again struck the hour, and since then the "Internationale" has rung out over Moscow. As has been the custom since the 15th century, clockmakers were hired to service the huge machinery in the Kremlin. The most recent general overhaul took place in 1974. The hands on Spasskaia Tower then stood still for three months until the 25-ton clockwork ran again, with several new parts. The 1918 wave of restoration activities was marked by the setting of definite goals and the simultaneous renovation of many monuments. In most of the decrees, regulations and instructions, the separate measures are seen as parts of a consequent scientific preservation program and a national duty.

Photographs taken in 1918, 1919, and 1920 show scaffolding on the towers and old cathedrals in the Kremlin. Several buildings were completely restored. Lenin constantly kept an eye on the renovation activities on Red Square and in the Kremlin, and he had lively discussions with the restorers in Uspenskii Cathedral. He watched the restoration of the old paintings in Vasilii Blazhenny Cathedral with interest. For Lenin, it was unthinkable to leave in the Kremlin such monuments as the statues of Alexander II, the obelisk at the place where an attempt was made on S. Romanov's life, and the tsar's coat of arms on the façade of the Grand Kremlin Palace. According to him, the Workers' and Farmers' Republic required new monuments and symbols to express the ideas and feelings of the workers. At the same

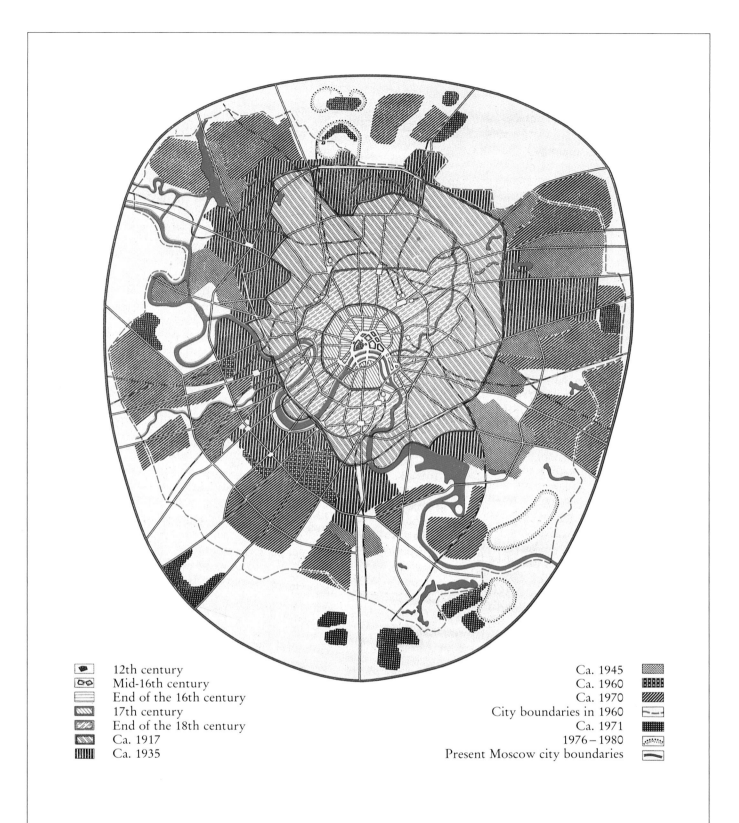

12th century			Ca. 1945	
Mid-16th century			Ca. 1960	
End of the 16th century			Ca. 1970	
17th century			City boundaries in 1960	
End of the 18th century			Ca. 1971	
Ca. 1917			1976–1980	
Ca. 1935			Present Moscow city boundaries	

Present area of modern Moscow and the ring freeway, the temporary border of settled areas. This growth sketch clearly indicates the increasing rate of expansion. The trunk roads surround the heart of the city in several concentric rings.

time, Lenin vigorously opposed tendencies to underestimate architectural and art monuments and to reject the nation's cultural and historical heritage. He told young people: "Proletarian culture can hardly develop out of nothing; it is also certainly not the invention of those who like to call themselves experts on proletarian culture. Both [ideas] are absolute humbug. A proletarian culture must represent the logical development of those stores of knowledge that humankind has been able to create and accumulate even under the yoke of capitalists, big landowners and civil servants."

The serious consequences of the civil war interrupted the restoration of the Kremlin for almost an entire decade (1921–1930). From 1931 to 1935 building activities were resumed, first on the southern section of the wall, facing the Moskva, between Peter Tower and the Water Tower. In addition, the northwest, from Troitskaia Tower to the Corner Arsenal Tower, was rebuilt. In 1932, work was begun on the towers facing Red Square and the wall between them. At the initiative of M. Kalinin, the head of state at that time, a "Committee for the Preservation of Monuments of the Revolution and Art" was founded at the Parliamentary Presidium in 1932. During restoration activities in 1935, the four huge double eagles, the former symbol of the tsars, were removed from the Spasskaia, Nikolskaia, Borovitskaia, and Troitskaia Towers, as were two eagles from the Historical Museum. In their place, five-pointed stars designed by F. Fedorovski and made of alloyed gilt steel and red copper sheets were mounted atop the towers. Unfortunately, the dirty metropolitan air robbed the stars of

their luster within only a year. They thus were replaced by stars made of ruby-colored glass and were illuminated from within. A fifth star was added to the Water Tower in 1937.

In 1940, repairs were being carried out on the section of the wall between Troitskaia Tower and Borovitskiia Gate along the Alexander Gardens. A commission introduced new plans and recommendations for the preservation and renovation of historical buildings and paintings in the Kremlin in December. Then the Germans invaded on June 22, 1941. During the first days of the war, emergency measures were decreed for the protection of the Kremlin. On October 19, the State Committee of Defense declared the capital to be in a state of siege. The stars of the towers were covered up and the golden domes of the churches and cathedrals, as well as the white wall sections of the palaces, were painted a dark color. The chimes in Spasskaia Tower were silenced – only the Moscow radio station continued to broadcast the striking of the hours. The treasures and library of the Armory were evacuated inland. When it became apparent in 1942–1943 that the tides of war were turning, the tradition arose of firing off salutes to military victories in the Kremlin. In May 1945, the ruby stars once again shone above the towers. On May 9, the salvos of the grand victory salute rang out over Moscow's rooftops. During the first few days after the end of the war, new plans were drawn up for the restoration of the Kremlin and its monuments. Also, within 40 days the Armory set up a new exhibition of the most important objects in nine halls.

A comprehensive restoration program for the entire Kremlin began in 1946 that eliminated the traces of war. The dark camouflage paint disappeared, as did the layers of dirt and paint from previous centuries. The Kremlin's brick walls were given a protective coating of PVC paint, and the socle was encased with white stone slabs. Seepage and drainage pipes were laid along the ring wall. The balconies were reopened in the towers, the coping and merlon surfaces of the walls were recoated, and the broken gutters and waterpipes were repaired everywhere. New red bricks were manufactured in the traditional Kremlin size according to old "recipes."

In the years following World War II, many Kremlin towers regained their old, festive splendor. The turquoise-colored glazed tiles of the roofs shimmered once again. Gilt weather vanes shone at their tips, and the gold-colored eaves lent them an air of gaiety. The missing decorations on Spasskaia Tower were recreated out of white stone according to old designs, as were statues. The white ornamental plasterwork on St. Nicholas Tower was completely repaired. Beklemishevskaia Tower and Corner Arsenal Tower were restored to their original medieval character as fortress-castle towers. The embrasures and machicolations, which had been widened into broad windows in the 18th century, and the levers and chains of the drawbridges and gates of Konstantin Yelena Tower were repaired. For the first time, the towers and ring wall were systematically measured and their ground plans drawn.

The five tower stars deserve special mention. In 1946, the illuminated stars created in 1937 were replaced by new ruby-colored ones made of three layers of convex glass (one ruby-colored, one transparent, and one milky-white layer) supported by a stainless steel skeleton. The statistics of these stars are impressive: 27.5 kilograms of gold for the copper frames for the glass, height between 3 and 3.78 meters, weight 1 to 1.5 tons per star. Ventilators cool the lamps, which illuminate the stars night and day with power outputs from 3,700 to 5,000 watts Complicated technical installations keep the interiors free of dust, snow, and condensation water.

The efforts to preserve the Kremlin national monument diminished only slightly in the decades following World War II. Entire armies of restorers, art historians, designers, engineers, physicists, and chemists have sought solutions to new problems in recent years. Time leaves its mark, even on a monument like the Kremlin. Old buildings and building materials are put to severe tests by a large, modern city. For this reason, a comprehensive research program to save threatened buildings in the Kremlin recently has been put into effect. In 1973, the first step of the reconstruction and renovation program for Red Square was begun, in which the wall and towers along the main square of the Soviet metropolis were restored. Old, weathered bricks were replaced and the new ones pointed with a cement mixture. The section of the wall between Spasskaia and Nikolskaia Towers was resurfaced inside and out with a water-resistant layer and painted a uniform color. The other towers were also subjected to an intensive "rehabilitation." The activities have not yet been completed, and already new tasks are waiting. Like so many other large architectural monuments, the Kremlin is a permanent building site.

Pages 68/69: View from the northeast of the Church of St. Basil and the fairytale illumination of the Moscow Kremlin at night.

The main monuments in the Moscow Kremlin:

1 Spasskaia or Savior Tower, most magnificent tower of the Kremlin fortifications. Erected by Pietro Antonio Solario in 1491. 67 meters high. Originally called Frolovskaia Tower, it was the main gate of the Kremlin. In 1658 the name was changed because of the Savior (*spas*) icon on the tower. See page 32.

2 Arsenal (Sobakin) Tower. Built by Pietro Antonio Solario near estate of the boyar Sobakin in 1492. Ca. 60 meters high. The superstructure was added in 1816 by the architect Bovet.

3 Troitskaia (Trinity) Tower. Built in 1495. 80 meters high. The name comes from the neighboring Troitski Monastery.

4 Kutafia Tower, now the official entrance to the Kremlin. Built as watchtower in 1495. It formerly stood in the Neglinnaia River and was protected on both sides by drawbridges. The superstructure, added in 1685, was considerably changed in 1867.

5 Borovitskaia Tower. Built in 1490 by P.A. Solario. 54 meters high. Large shipments for the farm buildings nearby were delivered at the gate.

6 Water-Pumping (Sviblov) Tower. Erected by Antonio Friazin in 1488. 59 meters high. It was destroyed in 1812 and rebuilt from 1817 to 1919 to its present form.

7 First Nameless Tower. 34 meters high. It was destroyed in 1770, rebuilt in 1783, blown up in 1812, and again rebuilt.

8 Peter Tower. 27 meters high. The name derives from the Church of Metropolitan Peter, once located in this tower.

9 Tsar Tower. Built in 1680. 17 meters high. A wooden tower is believed to have been located on this site previously.

10 Cathedral of the Assumption. Built from 1475 to 1479 by Aristotele Fioravante di Rodolfo. Interior paintings completed in 1515, renovated 1642–1643, houses an important icon collection, among others.

11 Cathedral of the Annunciation. Built 1484–1485 on top of older foundations by an architect from Pskov. Enlarged 1562–1564. The interior painting was done in 1508. Contains an important iconostasis.

12 Cathedral of the Archangel. Built by Alovisio Novo 1505–1508. Painting renovated 1652–1666. Houses, among other objects, over 50 sarcophagi of grand princes, tsars, and sons of tsars.

13 Palace of Facets. Built by Marco Ruffo and Pietro Antonio Solario 1487–1491. Painted 1668; completely renovated 1882.

14 Terem Palace. Built in the 16th century; stories added 1635–1636. Connected to the Grand Kremlin Palace in the 19th century, it is an excellent testimony to Old Russian architecture and interior design.

15 Grand Kremlin Palace. Built according to a design by Konstantin Andreyevich Thon from 1838 to 1849, it integrated older palace and church buildings (Terem Palace, Palace of Facets, Holy Vestibule, etc.).

16 Senate Building. Built according to drafts by Matvei Kasakov from 1776 to 1787, it now contains the Lenin Museum.

17 Arsenal. Construction started in 1701. Rebuilt after 1817, it holds a significant collection of old cannons along the eastern façade.

18 Armory. Built by Konstantin Andreyevich Ton 1844–1851 to replace medieval workshops and subsequent buildings. One of the largest museums from the 19th century, it is the heart of the Kremlin Museums and houses prominent collections.

19 Palace of Congress. Built 1960–1961.

20 Belfry of Ivan the Great. Built 1505–1508; stories added in 1600. Further enlarged in 1624, it is the highest building in the Kremlin.

21 Tsar Cannon. Cast in 1586, it is now located in front of the Church of the Twelve Apostles.

22 Tsar Bell.

23 Red Square.

24 Place of the Brow (former execution site).

25 Cathedral of St. Basil. Built 1555–1561.

26 Lenin Mausoleum. Built in 1930.

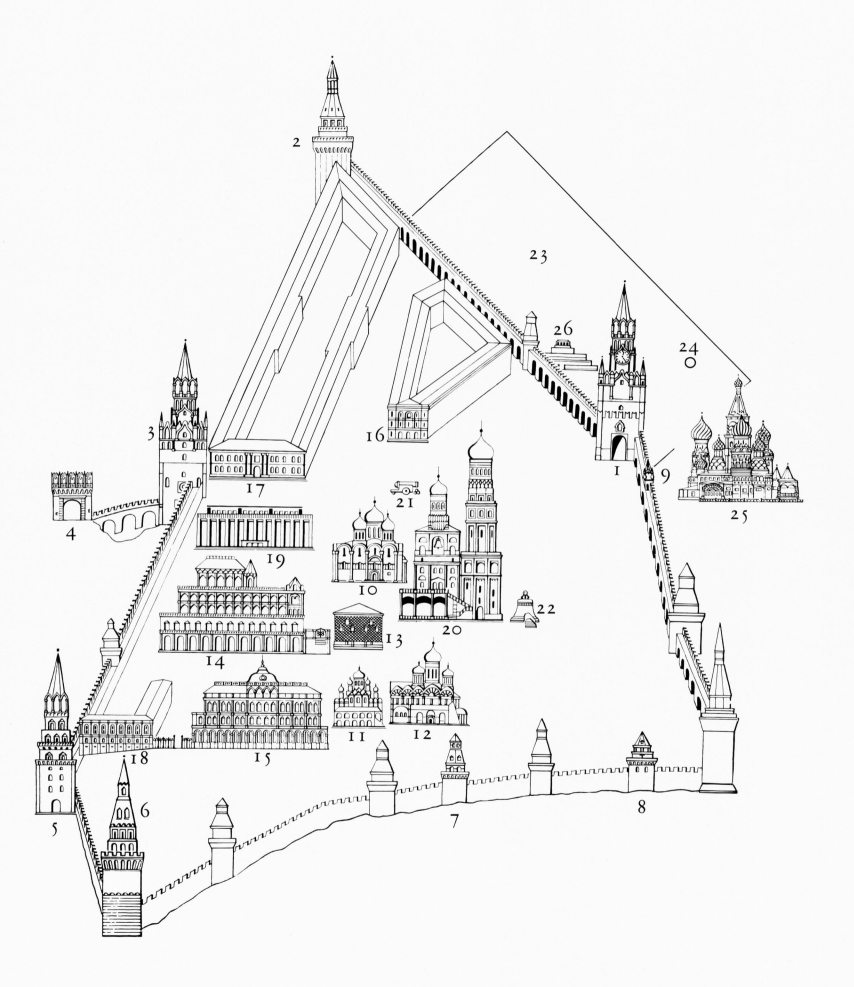

▷ Cathedral Square. Drawing from a book published in 1672. *The Election and Coronation of Grand Prince Michail Feodorovich as tsar*. Printed in 1856.

A Christian place of worship was probably located on Borovitskii Hill to the north of the Moskva, since fortifications were built there late in the 11th century. It seems likely that this place was on the top of the hill, in the middle of the present Kremlin grounds. According to the chronicles, when Khan Batu's hordes attacked Moscow in 1237–1238, the holy churches fell victim to the flames. Reconstruction was disturbed by a second Tatar assault in 1293, but soon thereafter, two wooden cathedrals stood in the Kremlin.

In 1326, the head of the Russian Church, Metropolitan Peter, moved the see from the old capital, Vladimir, to Moscow. In so doing, he decisively strengthened the authority of the young state led by the energetic Grand Prince Ivan Kalita. A rapid pace of church-building also set in at that time. In the same year, construction of the Cathedral of the Assumption was begun. Ivan Kalita created a spiritual focus in the center of his fortified court by building further churches and founding monasteries in the following years. The concentration of the various chapels, churches, and cathedrals on Borovitskii Hill that occurred at that time was to determine the basic layout of the future Cathedral Square.

However, the location did not take on its present appearance until Grand Prince Ivan III had the Kremlin enlarged into a Renaissance fortress. Between 1485 and 1508, all of the larger Kremlin buildings were either fundamentally altered or built anew. The upper terrace of Borovitskii Hill was designed in the nature of a magnificent piazza, and a unique ensemble of six large edifices was erected within a good 200-meter radius.

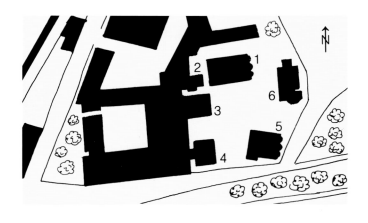

◁ Cathedral Square on the southeastern part of the Kremlin grounds. Six huge buildings surround it and form a unique complex: 1. The Cathedral of the Assumption (Uspenskii Sobor); 2. The Church of the Repository of the Robe (Tserkov Rizpolozhenia); 3. The Palace of Facets; 4. The Cathedral of the Annunciation (Blagoveshchenskii Sobor); 5. The Cathedral of the Archangel (Arkhangelskii Sobor); 6. The Belfry of Ivan the Great.

▷ The view from the Moskva toward the churches on Borovitskii Hill. At the foot of the terrace, the red wall and Tainitskaia Tower. Behind the tower, the impressive silhouette of the "City of God" culminating in the Belfry of Ivan the Great. At far left, the many domes of Blagoveshchenskii Cathedral.

▷ ▷ The gilt domes of the Terem churches.

74

The Cathedral of the Assumption

(Uspenskii Sobor)

The Cathedral of the Assumption was formerly the main church of Moscow and the Kremlin. The coronations of the grand princes were celebrated in this cathedral; metropolitans and patriarchs were installed and buried here. As of the 16th century, the tsar was crowned in the Cathedral of the Assumption.

The origin of this building is closely bound to the development of the Russian State. Immediately following the Russian metropolitan's move to Moscow in 1326, the cornerstone of the Cathedral of the Assumption was laid. The cathedral's patronage had already been bound to the seat of the patriarch when it was located in Vladimir. This original cathedral building was the first stone church in Moscow and, with only one dome, was not very large. It was designed completely in the Old Russian style. After 1395 it housed the miracle-working Image of St. Vladimir, a Russian national shrine.

After the Moscow Kremlin had risen to become the center of power and culture in the second half of the 15th century, the small, 14th-century Cathedral of the Assumption no longer seemed appropriate. Local architects began construction of a new church in 1471, which progressed to the vaults and then partially collapsed.

Ivan III then summoned Aristotele Fioravante di Rodolfo from Bologna (b. ca. 1415; d. ca. 1485, probably in a Moscow prison). The world-famous architect, engineer, bronze caster and medalist arrived in Moscow on April 20; within a week he had leveled the ruins. He then traveled to the former Russian capital, Vladimir, to study the 12th-century Cathedral of the Assumption there, which he had been directed to use as a model. Once back in Moscow, Fioravante had the Kremlin's new cathedral erected of better building materials, and it was dedicated on August 12, 1479. Its interior painting was completed in 1515. A fire broke out in the church in 1547; however, it did not cause very serious damage. The interior was slightly altered in the 17th century and was repainted in 1642–1643.

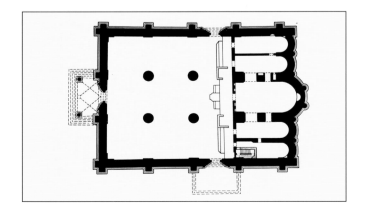

◁ Ground plan of the Cathedral of the Assumption.

▷ Portal and part of the south wall of the Cathedral of the Assumption. The introverted edifice, characterized by strict symmetry and compact mass, appeals to its surroundings at only a few places, such as the portals. In accordance with the old Russian tradition, the portals have several tiers and are embellished with paintings. Above the crown of the arch is the Head of Christ, flanked on the left by Archangel Michael and on the right by an angel writing; in the blind gallery, a row of patriarch-saints; under the arch, Maria Glicophiluza (the Caressing) and child, assisted by two angels.

The Cathedral of the Assumption stands on the north side of Cathedral Square. It surpasses all other Kremlin churches in size and magnificence, although its façade lacks opulence and grandeur. The five-cupola edifice has an elongated floor plan, a compact, massive shape, and a striking monumentality. Its walls, made of smooth, gray limestone blocks, rise in one sweep from the socle to the *zakomaras*, the typical curvature of the type of barrel roof in Russian cruciform-domed basilicas. Mighty lisenes, which receive the thrust of the vault, divide the long walls into four sections and the short sides into three.

The austereness of this stone shell probably sprang from the rationalistic mentality of engineer and bridge-builder Fioravante. An absolute symmetry prevails in the sequence of wall sections and projections. Heights and widths relate to each other in a harmony probably determined by the Golden Section. Although the richly adorned cathedral in Vladimir served as a model and its general form was imitated, the Moscow edifice almost completely lacks sculptured decorations and segmental divisions. The deeply stepped windows of Vladimir are reduced to extremely narrow apertures and the mighty, blind arcatures, to applied filigree ornamentation. The Bolognese architect avoided anything that might have emphasized the massiveness of the walls and led to superfluous externals. Even the apses of the east wall are flattened and pressed as far as possible into the main block of the building. And, because they project somewhat despite this, Fioravante had blind walls laid along their sides in order to retain the forceful shape of a cleanly cut cube.

Only in two sections does this absolutely introverted architecture appeal to the outside world: in the roof zone, dominated by the bulbous gilt domes, and at the round-arched portals, which possess the traditional multiple stepping and are embellished with paintings. The splendid porch on the west side, with its open loggia, was added later and does not conform to Fioravante's architectural concept. It remains to be clarified whether the outside walls were ever whitewashed like the drums of the cupolas, thereby presenting a friendlier appearance.

▷ The Cathedral of the Assumption as seen from the Belfry of Ivan the Great (from the southeast). The flattened apse wall can be distinguished clearly in this picture.

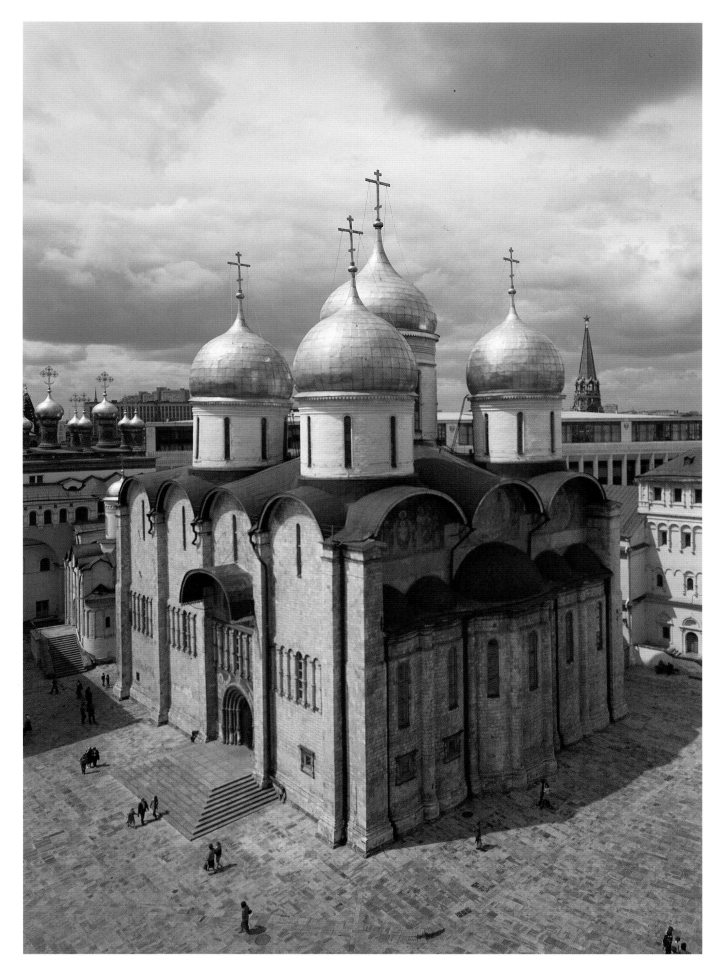

Upon entering the cathedral, the visitor is surprised by its well-lit vast space, its harmonious regularity, and the formal uniformity of its architectural elements. Fioravante, a mathematically skilled architect and engineer, undoubtedly was acquainted with the Renaissance churches in Mantua and Florence built only shortly before he went to work in Moscow. An extreme schematism and symmetry were applied in the ground plan. Fioravante divided the elongated rectangle into a grid with twelve squares and grouped these by means of three pairs of pillars into an ensemble of three naves. He set the five-domed roof atop the church in such a way that the hindmost bay at the west entrance remained free, whereas in the other bays the cross vaults and domed areas alternated with absolute symmetry. The entrance bay, which in contrast to the Russian architectural tradition has no choir, is fully integrated into the main hall. By applying improved building techniques, Fioravante was able to build bays wider than was usual for Old Russian churches. His contemporaries supposedly admired the hardness of the mortar, the thinness of the vault roofs, and the iron tie rods, which the Italian master builder used instead of the usual wooden supports to counteract the thrust of the vault. The slender circular columns in the central dome in front of the iconostasis emphasize the impression of endless width. The effect caused by not having built any secondary rooms to the west of the iconostasis is tremendous. Behind this large barrier to sight, everything is built on a smaller scale, the side aisles are divided longitudinally into two chapels, and the walls are set into the flanks of the main apse and walled up into the rectangular pillars near the iconostasis.

▷ The isometric proportions of the Cathedral of the Assumption. 1–10: Sarcophagi of Metropolitans Peter, Feognost, Kiprian, Photii, Iona, Gerontii, Simon, Makarii, Afanasii, Philipp II. 11–19: Tombs of the Patriarchs Iov I, Iermogen, Philaret, Nikitich (father of Tsar Mikhail Romanov), Ioasaph I of the 4th, Ioasaph V, Ioasaph II of the 7th, Pitirim VIII, Joachim IX, Adrian X. 20. Canopy by Master Desvershchkov. 21. Seat of the Tsar. 22. Seat of the Patriarch. 23. Throne of Monomakh. 24. Mensa. 25. Iconostasis. A. West portal and outdoor stairs. B. North portal. C. South portal. D/E. Peter and Paul Chapel. F. "Mount." G. High altar. H. Sacristy. I. Chapel of Dmitrii Solunski. K. Stairs to the Chapel of Praise of the Mother of God.

▷ ▷ View of the wide nave and pillars of the Cathedral of the Assumption. In the background, the iconostasis.

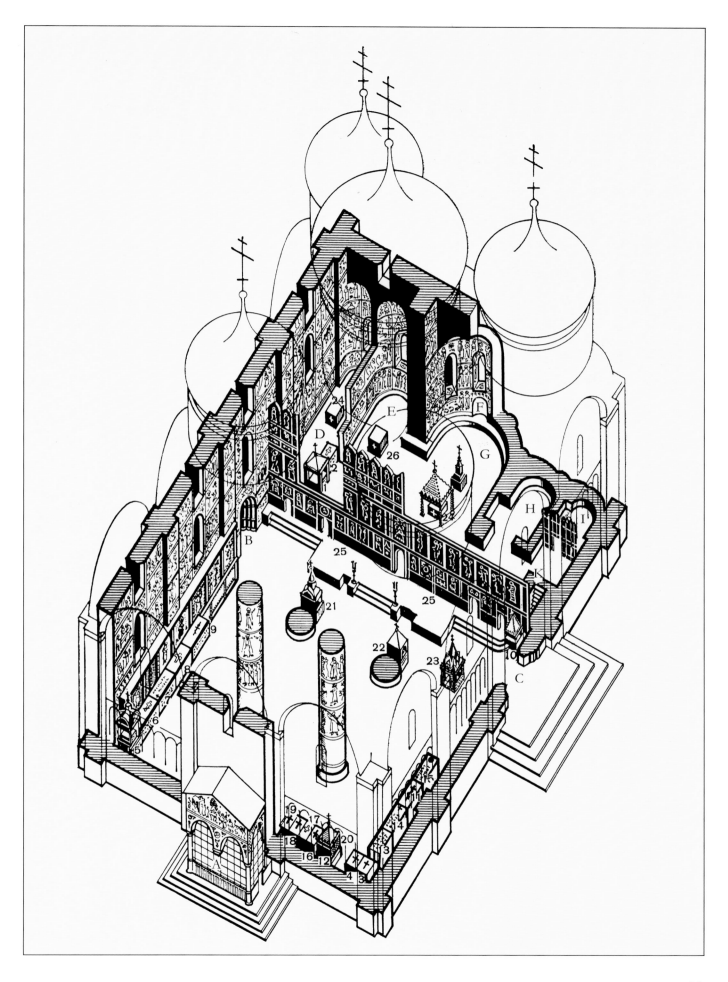

The iconostases of Orthodox churches developed out of the partition between the sanctuary and the nave. After the beginning of the 14th century, this partition bore a *deesis* (a portrayal of Christ between Mary and John the Baptist, who were presented in an attitude of intercession). Later, other pictures were added until the design of this art form was perfected around 1400. The iconostasis dominates the furnishings of Russian Orthodox churches. Three doors, the middle one called the Royal or Tsar's Door, lead into the sanctuary. The deesis reposes above the Royal Door amidst Apostles, archangels, and other saints – the main row of icons. Above it is a row of icons representing the festivals of the church. In large iconostases, another row of icons showing the prophets extends across the very top and a row of smaller ones is located below the main row. The lowest zone is reserved for special icons.

The first iconostasis for the Cathedral of the Assumption, for which Dionissius and his journeymen were given the commission in 1481, fell into ruin. In its place today stands an iconostasis with five rows of icons and 19th-century gilt frames. The icons in the upper four rows and the paintings on the doors were created by various Russian masters around the middle of the 17th century. Very valuable icons from different times and origins are contained in the bottom zone and in the shrine, including "St. George" (12th century, the oldest icon in the Cathedral of the Assumption, probably from Novgorod); "Trinity" (first half of the 14th century); "Redeemer with the Wrathful Eyes" (probably from the mid-14th century, Moscow School); "St. Michael" (first half of the 13th century); and "Metropolitan Peter" (around 1500, probably by Dionissisus).

▷ The "Madonna of Vladimir" icon. This painting, located in the Cathedral of the Assumption, was created at the beginning of the 15th century and is attributed to the circle around Andrei Rublev. It is a copy of a famous Byzantine icon from the 11th or 12th century that was brought to Vladimir in 1155 and later removed to Moscow. It is housed in the Tretyakov Gallery.

△ "The Redeemer with the Wrathful Eyes" icon. Created around the middle of the 14th century, probably by an icon painter from the Moscow court trained in Byzantium.

▷ "St. George" icon. Probably painted in Novgorod around 1100.

Page 90: An example of one of the many recent restorations: Medieval Mary icon while being cleaned. A dark layer of dirt still covers most of the picture. The "window" made by the restorer provides a glimpse of the splendid original surface.

Page 91: "Metropolitan Peter" icon. Painted toward the end of the 15th century, probably by Dionissius. The hagiographic work framed by 18 smaller pictures depicts the first Muscovite Metropolitan and scenes from his life.

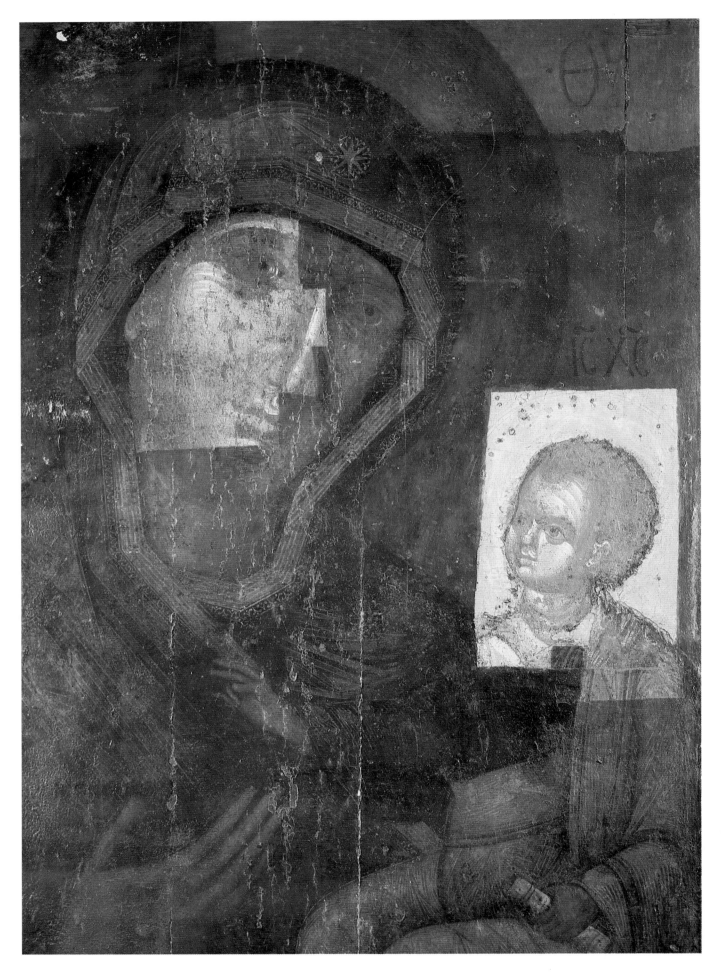

90

The first frescos were painted in the Cathedral of the Assumption as early as the 15th century. From 1513 to 1515, the great expanses of walls and ceiling were completely covered. 150 years later, they had suffered so greatly from fires and intensive use of the church that the only feasible solution was to paint them anew. Before the walls were destroyed in 1642, the old paintings were copied, according to the reports of that time. Then, numerous icon painters – supposedly there were over 100 – redecorated the cathedral, adopting the old system of pictures, division of wall areas, and probably also details of composition. In 1773 and again in the 19th century, the frescos were covered with oil paint. Restoration which was begun in 1911, but not completed, has only recently been continued.

The oldest existing frescos date from about 1481, when the famous painter Dionissius was awarded the commission for an iconostasis. On the masonry base of the wall, later covered with icons, approximately 20 figures of saints have been preserved. The regularity of the sequence and the clearly outlined, innerly serene figures painted in subdued shades indicate the hand of the master. Scenes located in the apses also can probably be attributed to Dionissius and the artists in his circle. These pictures include "The Forty Martyrs of Sebaste," "Apostle Peter Heals the Sick," and "The Seven Sleeping Youths of Epheseus" in the Peter and Paul Chapel; in the former Chapel of Laudation, "The Three Youths in Purgatory" and "The Adoration of the Magi"; and in the connecting passage to the Demetrius Chapel, "The Birth of John the Baptist."

The 1642 fresco, overflowing with figures, is a magnificent compendium of Old Russian faith. The rich coloring, with its warm, reddish-brown and yellow hues, and the strict dogmatism of the pictures must have created an atmosphere of religious fervor and impassioned festivity in combination with the powerful architecture of the cathedral's interior. In the cupolas, divine personages and the Mother of God appear, accompanied on the drum walls by angels, prophets, church dogmatists, apostles, and other saints. Several rows of cycles depicting many figures extend along the longitudinal walls: above, the life of Mary; in the middle, the glorification of the Mother of God; and at the bottom, seven scenes of ecumenical councils. They all begin at the south side of the iconostasis. Well over 100 figures of saints and martyrs adorn the pillars, window jambs, and reinforcing arches.

△ The Cathedral of the Assumption, longitudinal cross-section from west to east showing the scheme of interior paintings.

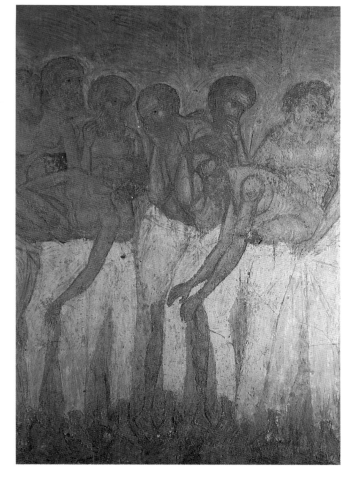

△ Inner south wall of the Peter and Paul Chapel in the Cathedral of the Assumption. "The Forty Martyrs of Sebaste." Painted in 1481 and attributed to the school of Dionissius. Subdued, light coloring and balanced movement of the figures. The marked differences in painting technique from the Pheodosius picture lead to the assumption that a different painter was at work here.

Pages 94/95: Cathedral of the Assumption, view of the central section of the north wall showing the row of icons on the socle and two rows of paintings from the 16th century (below, a row of scenes from councils; above, scenes from the life of Mary; on the columns, saints).

Page 96: Cathedral of the Assumption, inner west wall. The "Last Judgment" section of the frescos. According to Old Russian legends about this event, the hopes for the mercy of the judges and an afterlife in a world of justice and goodness were emphasized. Therefore, the Old Russian representations of the Last Judgment are friendlier and more peaceful than, for example, the Western European visions

of horror. The Brazen Snake twists through the center of the Last Judgment, which was painted on the west wall in the 16th and 17th centuries. Above the snake, Christ triumphs in the mandorla. John and Mary prostrate themselves before him, and the choirs of saints and the beatified stand at his sides.

Page 97: Iconostasis in the Cathedral of the Assumption. Representation of St. Feodosii the Great. A fresco from the original iconostasis, the stone base of which has been preserved underneath younger icons. Painted in 1481, school of Dionissius.

ΟΑ ΔΕWCIC   ΟΑ ΙСΑСΥΡΗΙ

The Cathedral of the Annunciation

(Blagoveshchenskii Sobor)

On the southern part of Cathedral Square, the Cathedral of the Annunciation rises on the edge of the Kremlin hill. It is another of the impressive architectural monuments from the 15th century. When the slightly older previous building (built 1397–1416) on this site was torn down in 1482 because of its ruinous state, the high, natural stone socle remained standing. From 1484 to 1489, master builders from Pskov erected a cubical brick edifice on top of it with three apses and an exterior gallery on three sides, which for a time remained open. They placed a mighty drum cupola atop the nave and two flanking cupolas over the side apses. The cathedral retained its original form until the mid-16th century, when, after a fire in 1547, Ivan the Terrible had the edifice renovated and expanded from 1562 to 1564. To make the building symmetrical, the side cupolas on the eastern side were balanced with counterparts on the western side of the same shape, although they were blind – that is, they did not open up into the interior of the cathedral. A fourth leg was built to close up the gallery extending along three sides of the church and a ring of chapels added on top of it. Four corner domes were built onto this addition. In the 1570s, an annex with an outdoor stairway was erected on the south wall at the request of Ivan the Terrible.

The cathedral's extremely picturesque appearance results from the variety of architectural shapes, the smallness of the parts that make up its graceful decorations, and the festive display of gold and white. On the three apses facing Cathedral Square on the central part of the building, there are a dwarf, blind balustrade high up on the wall and a sequence of arcades made of spiral columns applied to the wall. Several tiers of gilt decorative arches (*kokoshniks*) rise above the semiconical roofs to the cupola bases. The motif of blind arcades, which probably was imported from Vladimir, is repeated on the drums of the cupolas. The frieze on the drums has a much more intricate design than the one on the walls of the cubical element. The circular bands of zigzag friezes, the billet friezes, and the stepped arches lie like filigree on the walls and make a splendid display together with the decorative golden bands encircling the foot of the bulbous domes. Undoubtedly, these very graceful ornaments reminiscent of chip carvings come from the home of the Pskov architects. Next to them, the

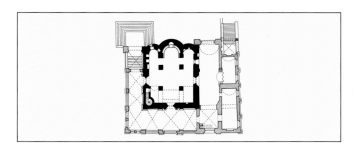

◁ Ground plan of the Cathedral of the Annunciation.

△ The Cathedral of the Annunciation from the northwest. The original building with its three apses (built 1484 – 1489) is easily distinguishable from the superstructures (built 1562 – 1564) above the side galleries in the evening rays of light on a winter's day. At the far left is the stairway built in the 16th century. The formal differences between the 15th-century middle domes and the lateral pair of cupolas in the cool, classicist shape are visible on the roof.

▷ ▷ View of a side gallery, formerly open (on the left, the west flank; on the right, the north side), with frescos from the early 15th century to around 1520. Among other things, scenes from the life of Jonas are depicted on the blind arch to the left (the Prophet is being swallowed by the whale and then spit out on land). A climbing vine is painted on the vault, framing prophets, heads of clans, and disciples; individual scenes from the Old and New Testaments; the Tree of Jesse; and idealized portraits of antique writers and philosophers such as Virgil, Plato, and Homer. At the far left is a picture of the Savior painted by Simon Ushakov in 1661.

99

additions to the cathedral radiate a classicist coolness with their coffered walls and slightly projecting neckings. They flank the central part of the building with their small ogee-arched gables in a successful blend of Pskovian tradition and eclectic Muscovite court art. The Cathedral of the Annunciation served as the private chapel of the Muscovite princes. Built near the Palace of Grand Princes, it was the scene of several solemn ceremonies. The cave-like rooms of the cellar and its metal-clad portals housed the treasury of the Grand Prince, the state insignia, and the archives. It sometimes also served as a dungeon for particularly dangerous political prisoners. During recent archaeological studies, traces of older buildings were often found in this part of the Kremlin.

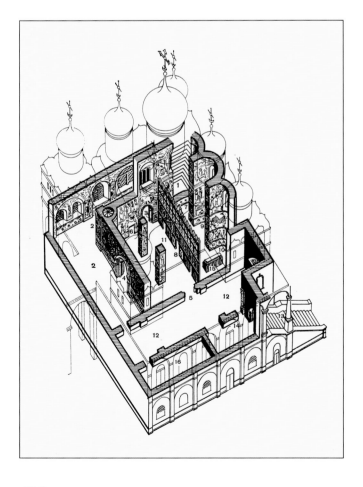

◁ Isometric representation of the Cathedral of the Annunciation: 1. Stairway to the porch; 2. Porch; 3. North portal; 4. West portal; 5. South portal; 6. Staircase to the choirs; 7. Mensa; 8. Tsar's Door; 9. Main altar; 10. Diaconicon; 11. Iconostasis; 12. Chapel of Nicholas the Miracle-Worker; 13. Stairway of Ivan the Great; 14. Porch; 15. Reliquary; 16. Sacristy.

▷ West portal of hewn and painted limestone, made at the beginning of the 16th century. Rich, plant-shaped ornamentation adopted from the Early Italian Renaissance covers the portal, which combines the Classic style (pairs of Corinthian columns with massive entablatures) with Russian architectural motifs (horseshoe arches).

The nucleus of the Cathedral of the Annunciation impresses one by its simplicity. Four slender, square columns – one pair is hidden by the iconostasis – surround the center of the interior. In this small church, they rise to an apparently endless height where the base of the central cupola admits light. Side barrel vaults, indicated on the exterior by the ogee-arched *kokoshniks* (recessive rows of corseled arches) receive the thrust of the vault and transfer it to the outer walls. Because it was a court church, the Cathedral of the Annunciation was specially furnished with a choir, which extends between the western bays and is connected to the prince's residence.

The frescos, which cover almost every inch of the interior, have been restored since 1947. According to written sources, they date from 1508. Most of them were probably created by Feodossi, the son of the famous Dionissius. However, different painting techniques indicate that other masters also worked on them.

The dome surfaces are covered with half-figures of the Pantocrator, the Mother of God, the prophets, apostles, archangels, and other holy figures. Along the wall of the apses appear eucharistic representations (in the main apse), Biblical scenes (in the north apse), events from the lives of Saints Basil the Great and Chrysostomus, and figures of saints. Feodossi's personal style of painting is most clearly evident in the paintings of the sanctuary: elongated figures in gently flowing robes move vigorously, yet harmonically, between and in front of artistically arranged architectural elements. The colors are brilliant, light, and rich. Soft contours, never faltering, reveal the hand of the master and his elegant, courtly style.

In the nave in front of the iconostasis, the walls are decorated with apocalyptic visions and the Last Judgment. These pictures, overflowing with figures, lack the preciseness of Feodossi's paintings but are of an absorbing intensity. The figures of rulers on the columns, on the other hand, more closely resemble Feodossi's artistic style.

▷ Inside room of the Cathedral of the Assumption. View of the southwest pillar with its built-in choir. Paintings from 1508. On the pillar in the foreground, the imperial couple Konstantin and Helena with the miracle-working cross; above them, the Second Horseman of the Apocalypse on a red horse and the Archangel showing the Book. In the background, below left, among others, a scene of Paradise; the founders of clans are pictured on the arch; to the right of them, the Last Judgment. At the above right on the pillar, a row of saints; below them, St. George and St. Dmitri Zolunski.

Page 106, top: Drum vault in the nave. Picture of Jesus Christ; under him, the heavenly hosts.

Page 106, bottom: Blind arch above the exit. The Manifestation of Archangel Michael. The dark spot at the lower edge shows the condition of the paintings before restoration.

Page 107: The philosopher Virgil. The cutout section at the right displays the layers of the painting down to the brick wall.

Characteristically enough, the Cathedral of the Annunciation immediately became a place where masterpieces of Old Russian painting were collected after it was turned into a museum. After all, this was only the continuation of an old tradition: icons from the church that formerly stood on this site were brought to the present cathedral (built 1484–1489). The icons in the church festival row to the left of the north wall and those of Archangel Michael in the second row have been identified as works of the great Rublev. They are characterized by harmonic colors and a refined rhythmical arrangement, which are typical of this ingenious artist.

Most of the icons were created by Theophanos the Greek, who tended to produce an effect of vast spaciousness and painted uncommonly large icons. The contours of his figures here thus appear softer and more balanced than those in his earlier Novgorod frescos. The latter's monochrome coloring has given way to tasteful color combinations in which each color supports another, yet also contrasts advantageously with it.

The third row of icons is attributed to Prokhor of Gorodets. They reveal a straightforward composition, fine linear rhythm, and complex color scheme. In the 16th century, artists from Pskov created the upper row of icons. Of particular artistic value are the icons in the first row, which consists of works in the Old Russian and Byzantine styles from several centuries. Among the icons dating from the beginning of the 14th century, those of the Hodegetria Mother of God and the Savior on the Throne are exceptionally noteworthy.

The wall of icons was completed in the 19th century, when art metalworkers from Moscow created an impressive encasing of gilt copper adorned with colorful enamel ornaments.

▷ △ The iconostasis in the Cathedral of the Annunciation. The oldest remaining multi-tiered iconostasis in the classic style found in the Moscow Kremlin. The chronicles report that Theophanos the Greek, Prokhor of Gorodets, and Andrei Rublev started work on the wall paintings and icons of this church in 1405. The icons in the deesis row are located high above the floor for good visibility. The upper part was made more recently (before the 19th century).

▷ Plan of the iconostasis: 1. God the Father; 2. The Mother of God; 3. The Annunciation; 4. The Birth of Christ; 5. The Circumcision; 6. Offering in the Temple; 7. The Epiphany; 8. The Transfiguration of Christ; 9. The Resurrection of Lazarus; 10. Entering Jerusalem; 11. The Last Supper; 12. The Crucifixion; 13. The Burial; 14. Christ in Limbo; 15. The Ascension; 16. The Pentecost; 17. The Assumption; 18. Basil the Great; 19. Apostle Peter; 20. Archangel Michael; 21. The Mother of God; 22. The Redeemer; 23. John the Baptist; 24. Archangel Gabriel; 25. Apostle Paul; 26. John Chrisostomus; 27. Nicholas the Miracle-Worker; 28. The Mother of God; 29. Archangel Uriel; 30. The Redeemer; 31. Hodegetria Mother of God framed by medallions of the progenitresses; 32. The Redeemer; 33. The Annunciation; 34. John the Baptist; 35. Archangel Raphael; 36. The Redeemer of Smolensk; 37. The Only Begotten Son of God.

112

113

A chronicle dating from the beginning of the 15th century underlines the particular importance of the Cathedral of the Annunciation for life at the Grand Prince's court in Moscow. This is why the best painters of the period – Theophanos the Greek, Prokhor of Gorodets, and, last but not least, Andrei Rublev – were entrusted with the decoration of its walls and iconostasis. Later, art experts claimed that these original icons from the 15th century had been lost to art, especially because the chronicles reported that they had been destroyed by the flames of the terrible city fire of 1547. During the first Soviet restoration, which began in 1918, great importance was attached to the systematic removal of the covering paintings applied later. This led to a sensational discovery: icons by famous Russian painters of the Middle Ages such as Andrei Rublev, Theophanos the Greek, and Prokhor of Gorodets proved to be fairly well preserved, and experts were able to restore them to excellent condition.

Later, restoration was carried on step by step under the necessary competent guidance. The more recent layers of paint were removed, millimeter by millimeter, from the icons and frescos. Since the 1940s, restorers from Moscow and painters from Palekh (a small, central Russian city known for its folk-art enamel painting) have worked on exposing and preserving the original paintings. This unique architectural and cultural monument has been the subject of research and restoration since the 1970s.

Pages 110/111: Icons from the left-hand side of the row of festivals. Left, Archangel Gabriel's Prophecy to Mary; right, the Birth of Christ. From the old iconostasis dating from 1405. Both paintings are attributed to Andrei Rublev.

Page 112: Icon of Archangel Michael from the deesis row. Attributed to Rublev.

Page 113: Icon of John the Baptist from the deesis row. Attributed to Theophanos the Greek.

▷ View of Cathedral Square from the Belfry of Ivan the Great. In the background, the Cathedral of the Annunciation.

The Church of the Repository of the Robe of Mary

(Tserkov Rizpoloshenye)

The present church was erected from 1484 to 1485 on the foundation of the previous church, built in 1451 and destroyed by fire in 1473. Metropolitan Gerontii hired a Pskov workshop, which had also worked on the Cathedral of the Annunciation, to erect the new church. Around the middle of the 17th century, alterations were carried out.

This architectural jewel is overshadowed by Uspenskii Cathedral and the Palace of Facets. The main body of the church, built as a cruciform-domed basilica with four central pillars, presents an extremely graceful exterior. A sharply designed block rises above the high socle. Mighty pilasters frame its edges and divide the façade into three sections, the middle one of which is accentuated. A blind terracotta balustrade with a palmette frieze divides the round-arched windows from the ground floor. In the west, a broad flight of stairs leads up to the multi-tiered, ogee-arched portal. All four fronts are topped off by a trio of ogee-arched zakomaras; the middle one is wider and taller and has a blind arcature on the entrance side of the church. An octagonal pedestal rises above the zakomaras, in accordance with Pskov tradition. It bears the cupola drum, which is adorned with the same carved stone frieze pattern as the main cupola of the Cathedral of the Annunciation.

▷ The Church of the Repository of the Robe as seen from outside. It is located on the northwest corner of Cathedral Square between the Chamber of Facets and the Uspenskii Cathedral. In the foreground, the passage to the Grand Kremlin Palace can be seen; in the background is Uspenskii Cathedral. The patronage of the repository of the chasuble originated with the worship of the Mother of God's robes, a cult that reached the height of its popularity in Russia in the mid-16th century.

Inside, the cave-like intimacy imparted by the Church of the Repository of the Robe charms the visitor. Slender rectangular pillars support the barrel vaults that rise to the central cupola. The dim light admitted by the four apertures in the domes and the narrow side windows tempers the breathtaking height of the vault.

The solemn atmosphere and sense of security is generated to a great degree by the paintings covering the entire surfaces of the walls, vaults, domes, and pillars. The murals were created in 1643–1644 by the icon painters Sidor Pospeyev, Ivan Borissov, and Simon Abramov. The first two artists had already assisted in painting the Uspenskii Cathedral. The paintings in the Church of the Repository of the Robe are done in bright, rich colors. A solid schematism characterizes the compositions. The figures clothed in tersely drawn robes impart a spirited sense of movement and are set against strongly staggered backgrounds.

▷ A view of the iconostasis and the vault above it. As the private church of the patriarchs, the Church of the Repository of the Robe was furnished strictly according to canonical rules. The murals conform to this framework. God the Father hovers in the cupola above the iconostasis. Prophets and evangelists are painted on the walls of the drum. The vertical walls display scenes from the life of the Mother of God and allegorical laudations of her name. Monks are pictured on the window reveals. The particularly comprehensive depiction of the life of the Mother of God in this church is taken from the Gospels of the Apocrypha.

△ Paintings on the flattened cupola over the high altar, created in 1643–1644, painted over with oil paints in the mid-19th century, exposed from 1955 to 1965, and then restored. The scene portrays the preparations for the repositing of the robe. The eucharistic symbols (the body of Jesus as a child and the blood of Jesus in the symbolic chalice) are being carried to the altar. Byzantine ritual and the splendor of the court mark the ceremony. Angels carry the liturgical implements to the three celebrants. God the Father, the Holy Ghost in the guise of a dove, and a six-winged seraphim hover over the scene.

▷ View of the west wall and into the vault above. In the bottom row are the Annunciation, the Birth of Jesus, the Journey of the Three Magi, and their Adoration of the Infant Jesus. The chandelier of gilt silver was made by Dmitrii Sverchkov from the Armory in 1624; it was restored in 1955–1956.

120

In 1955 and 1956 more recent paintings covering the originals were removed, and the originals were treated to preserve them. At the same time, the iconostasis created in 1627 by Nazari Isomin-Zavin, a member of the Stroganov school, was restored. Fresh, luxuriant colors, richly decorated silver frames, and a fine painting technique justify counting this icon wall among the most significant works of the first half of the 17th century. The art historical value of the Church of the Repository of the Robe is not least determined by the fact that the murals and icons were created in virtually the same period and can therefore convey a uniform, unadulterated impression of the figures and art of the 17th century. As in all the churches and cathedrals of the Kremlin, the interior of the Church of the Repository of the Robe was adorned with numerous products of the applied arts, yet all that remains are two painted candelabra inlaid with colored wax which were made in 1643–1645 at the request of Patriarch Iosif.

The northern gallery of the Church of the Repository of the Robe houses the exhibition "Folk sculpture and small statues." This art form, the origins of which go back to the most ancient folklore, has now almost disappeared, as it was forbidden and virtually destroyed by a strict synod decree in the 18th century. The figures of St. George (15th century) and an ancient Christian prophet (17th century) are vivid and expressive, well complemented by carefully made pictures of saints, icons, and crosses, and invaluable as a testimony to the astonishing, unique art of the unknown Russian craftsmen.

▷ △ Central icon: The Repository of the Robe. The scene is located in the Byzantine city of Blahern, where, according to legend, the Mother of God was born. The icon dates from the 17th century.

▷ ▷ △ Carved and painted icon of Nicholas of Moshaisk, the patron saint of trade. The icon dates from the 17th century.

▷ Wooden statue "Metropolitan Iona," from the 17th century.

▷ ▷ The "Fat Candle," with a wood core covered with wax. It is partially painted and partially inlaid with different shades of wax. Created around 1643–1645. A very rare specimen.

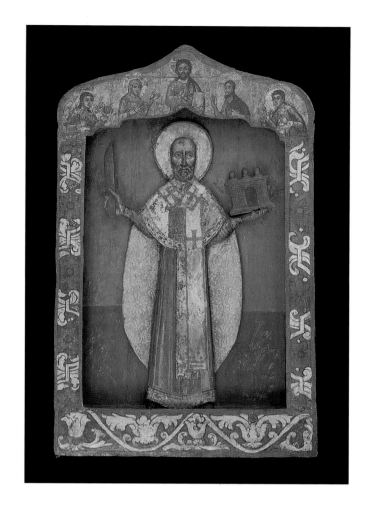

The Cathedral of the Archangel Michael

(Arkhangelskii Sobor)

It is said that a church dedicated to the Archangel Michael stood atop Borovitskii Hill in the southeast corner of Cathedral Square as early as the 13th century. Ivan Kalita had a church built of white stone on the same site in 1333 to serve as a burial place for the Muscovite princes. In 1505, Ivan III commissioned Alovisio Novo, an architect who had emigrated from Italy, to build a new cathedral. It was completed in 1508. The 16th-century paintings (probably from 1564–1565) were replaced by new ones in 1652–1666; many changes were also made on the exterior of the edifice. At the end of the 16th or beginning of the 17th century, the Chapels of St. Uara and John the Baptist were added to the east side. Large vertical fissures appeared in the south wall of the cathedral when building of the Grand Kremlin Palace was begun in 1773; they were stabilized by means of massive flying buttresses. At the same time, an arcaded gallery extending on three sides was removed, which permanently changed the appearance of the cathedral.

The monumental building is marked by the great order of Italian Renaissance architecture. Mighty pilasters with composite capitals decorated with feather motifs and angular cornices frame and divide the two-story, whitewashed façades. The lower story, atop a socle as tall as a man, makes a powerful figure and has a blind arcature that contrasts with the rectangular sections of the smaller upper story. The architect placed huge scallop-shell ornaments in the spandrels of the zakomaras above the entablature.

The two-story pilaster system serves as mere exterior decoration and has no relation to the interior, except for the two rows of windows. This makes all the more astounding the great synthesis Alovisio Novo succeeded in applying to the façade of the Cathedral of the Archangel: on the one hand, the multiple stepping of the wall surfaces and the pronounced pilasters and moldings give the impression of forming a segmented composition, and on the other hand, they emphasize the massiveness of the walls. The north and west portals have been given a special accent. Their window jambs are covered with brightly colored, partly

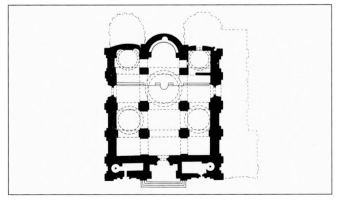

◁ Ground plan of the Cathedral of the Archangel Michael. See also the isometric sketch on page 130.

▷ View of the Cathedral of the Archangel from the Belfry of Ivan the Great, to the north. The pronounced division of the façade into irregular bays, the huge scallop-shell zakomaras, and the choir annexes on the apses of the east front are clearly visible in this photograph. In the background, the Cathedral of the Annunciation.

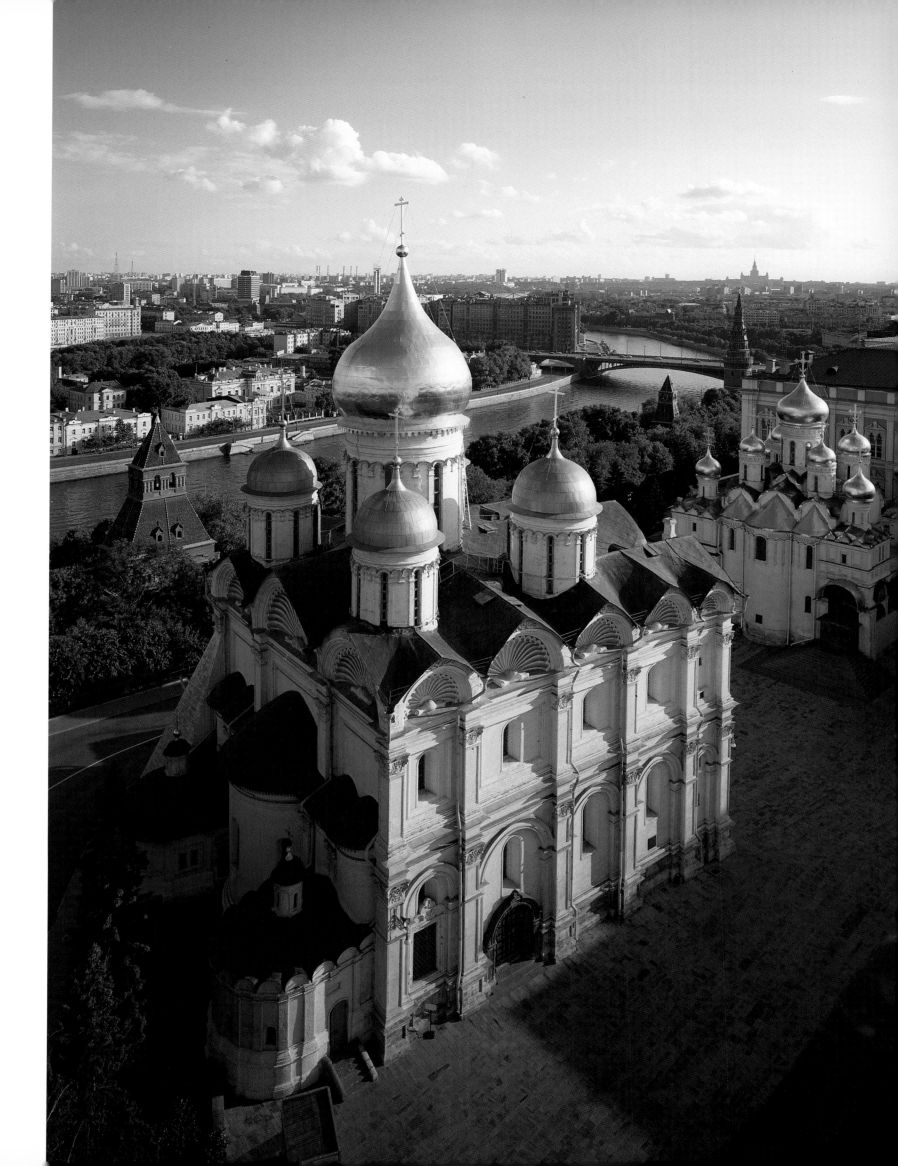

gilt ornaments. In addition, frescos on the theme of the Christianization of Russia embellish the loggia-like entrance.

The magnificent, solemn interior decorations of the Cathedral of the Archangel were executed in the Old Russian tradition. Six free-standing columns support the five-domed roof. Four of them are located in the nave, the other two in the sanctuary behind the iconostasis. As is the case in Uspenskii Cathedral, the main cupola rises above the iconostasis. The secondary domes are arranged in a cross around the central cupola. However, the Venetian Alovisio Novo designed barrel vaults for his building, unlike the architect of Uspenskii Cathedral, Fioravante. He arranged the brick columns in the pattern of a cross and set them atop high pedestals. Their pilasters continue in one line over the transverse arches to the engaged piers.

This results in a completely different feeling of space than that created by the mighty round pillars in the wide nave of Uspenskii Cathedral. In comparison, the pillar arrangement in the Cathedral of the Archangel is bound relatively closely to the vault and walls and divides the interior into a system of passages, wall elements, barrel vaults, and cupolas. The smallness of the individual parts and the harmonious proportions are well balanced here. At the same time, the Venetian architect successfully integrated the traditional Russian five-dome design with elements of Venetian palace architecture.

The interior of the Cathedral of the Archangel was probably painted in 1564–1565. Parts of this layer have been preserved in the altar area (primarily on the south apse) and in the porch of the west portal. The rest of the paintings were removed in 1652–1666 and recreated under the direction of the masters Simon Ushakov and Stepan Ryazanets by icon painters from Yaroslavl, Kostroma, and Valogda. Apparently, the motifs of the old, decayed paintings were carefully noted or even traced before their destruction, and the painters of the new icons followed the motifs and compositions indicated by these records.

More than 60 idealized portraits of Russian princes on the socle form an impressive gallery. Rulers who rendered the centralized state special services are pictured here, including Andrei Bogolubskii (the son of Iurii Dolgorukii); Yaroslav Vzevolodovich and his son Alexander Nevskii, the great Russian military leader under whose leadership the battles on the Neva and at Lake Chudskoye were won; and Daniil Alexandrovich, the founder of the feudal principality of Moscow. On the south wall, the Muscovite grand princes buried in the

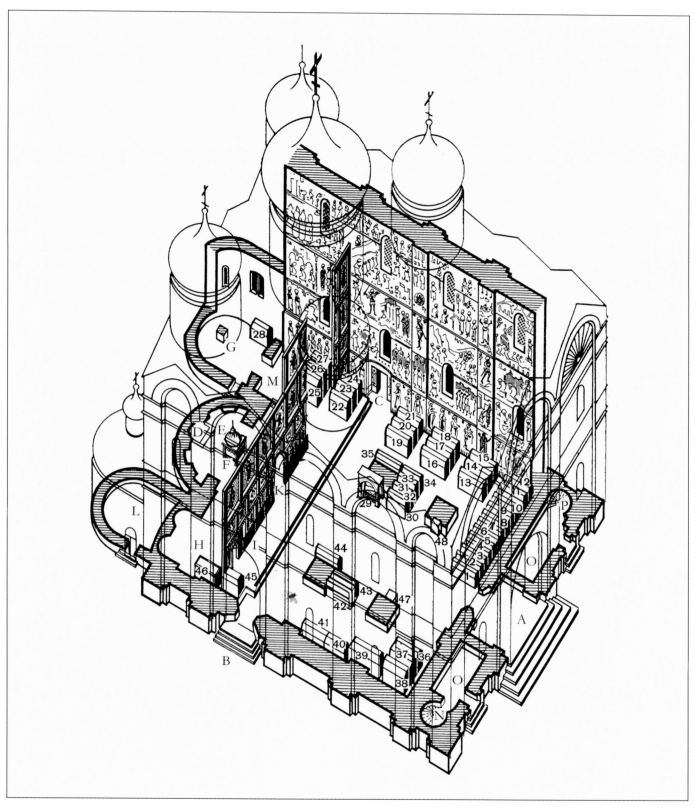

△ Isometric plan of the Cathedral of the Archangel. 1–48: Tombs of the grand princes, tsars, sons of tsars, and princes. Including: 23. Ivan III; 27. Ivan IV (the Terrible); 29. Tomb of False Dmitrii; 44. Tsar Peter II; A West portal; B. North portal; C. South portal; D. Mensa; E. "Mount"; F. High altar; G. Mensa; H. Diaconicon; I. Iconostasis; K. Tsar's Door; L. Chapel of St. Uara; M. Chapel of St. John the Baptist; N. Staircase to the loft; O. Furnace room; P. Storage room.

Page 128: View of the south wall and iconostasis. Its carved and gilt wooden parts were restored in accordance with the Moscow art school of the late 17th century after Napoleon's 1813 military campaign. Chandelier: Russian artwork from the 17th century.

Page 129: View from the northwest corner of the Cathedral of the Archangel, toward the entrance.

△ Cathedral of the Archangel Michael. Longitudinal section showing the scheme of frescos on the north wall.

▷ Section of the Last Judgment on the west wall: Peter opening the gates to Paradise for the Blessed.

131

cathedral are depicted in life size. Their long, wide robes are decorated with rich, gold-colored plant ornaments that harmonize with the decor on the windows and portals of the cathedral and produce a decorative, festive effect. The focus on historical figures in the interior decoration can be explained by the fact that this cathedral was seen as a symbol of a unified central state from the very beginning.

The vertical walls contain four rows of paintings above the portrait gallery on the socle. Among others, the west wall boasts a monumental Last Judgment surrounded by programmatic representations of the profession of faith. Countless figures fill the window jambs, barrel vaults, reinforcing arches, and cupolas, most of them portrayed in the traditional arrangement and canonical character. They comprise the most complete and comprehensive interior painting scheme in the churches of the Moscow Kremlin, even if it is not the most valuable from an artistic perspective. Archangel Michael dominates the many-figured scenes on the side walls. The highlights of this tremendous legendary world are two paintings of battles ("Gideon Defeats the Midionites" on the south wall and "Victory over the Assyrian Army" on the north). Scenes from the New Testament and the legend of Emperor Constantine are depicted on the lower sections of the side walls.

The Cathedral of the Archangel's 16th-century iconostasis has not been preserved. In 1680–1681 Dorofei Yermolayev Zalotaryov, Michail Yelutin, and Feodor Zubov, together with other master artists, created a new wall of pictures. It was renovated in 1813. The splendid upper section displays an unadulterated Russian baroque style with its returned moldings and spiral columns hung with a heavy grape pattern. Most of the icons come from the hands of the painters named above. The pictures in the festival row reveal a new feeling of corporality and a modern sense of space, thus ushering in the end of the Old Russian style of icon painting. The panel depicting the Archangel Michael and his life stand out among the older icons in the first row. Created in a Moscow school at the end of the 14th or beginning of the 15th century, the central picture shows the winged archangel with a sword, breastplate, and magnificent red cape. The 18 secondary pictures, depicting scenes from the Old Testament, are reminiscent of Rublev's style. It is said that Yefrozinya, the widow of Prince Dmitrii Donskoy, ordered these icons.

From the beginning of the 15th century until the first quarter of the 18th century, the Muscovite grand princes and, later, the tsars were interred in the Cathedral of the Archangel

▷ Central panel of the icon of Archangel Michael and his life.

132

Michael. The tradition was begun with Ivan Kalita (d. 1342) and continued by Dmitrii Donskoy, Grand Prince Ivan III, and Tsar Ivan the Terrible and his sons, as well as the first tsars of the Romanov dynasty, Michail Feodorovich and Alexei Michailovich. The Cathedral of the Archangel houses a total of 46 tombs containing 52 graves and two reliquaries. In 1636 and 1637 the brick sarcophagi were encased with white limestone engraved with decorative inscriptions in Russian and elegantly embellished frames. They have stood in glass cases with copper frames since 1903.

The tomb of Ivan the Terrible and his sons occupies a special position near the cathedral altar. When archaeological studies were started in the cathedral in 1963–1964, a special commission had the sepulchers investigated. New architectural details of the original inner construction of the grave, as well as of the auxiliary altar of John the Baptist nearby, were discovered. It proved possible to expose and preserve the fresco dating from the second half of the 16th century located on the lower part of the tomb. The opening of the sarcophagus also revealed the solution to several historical puzzles; for example, the exact date of Ivan the Terrible's death could at last be determined (March 18, 1584). Mikhail Mikhailovich Gerassimov, a well-known Soviet anthropologist, was able to produce true-to-life portraits of Ivan the Terrible and his son Feodor Ivanovich on the basis of skulls and bones found in the tombs.

A special location was also reserved for the grave of Ivan the Terrible's son Tsarevich Dmitrii, who died under mysterious circumstances as a child. It rests behind a decorative filigree grille under a canopy borne by artistically carved columns. The grave's silver ledger, now located in the Armory, boasts masterfully cast bas-reliefs and was created in 1630 in G. Odokonov's workshop.

During the course of renovation activities around 1980 it was possible to reproduce the original form of the façade, the painted portals, and four smaller cupolas; to secure the iconostasis; and to examine the condition of the tombstones. In order to better conserve the frescos, a heating system was installed in the Cathedral of the Archangel – as in all other cathedrals in the Moscow Kremlin – that guarantees a constant temperature and humidity during summer and winter.

▷ △ Sanctuary of the Cathedral of the Archangel, tomb of Ivan the Terrible and his sons. In the foreground, a bust of the tsar designed by anthropologist M. Gerassimov on the basis of skull fragments recently found in the tomb.

▷ South gate showing detail of the lock and bar. Silver- and gold-plated iron fittings with mythological beasts engraved on the bar (lions, centaur, unicorn).

The Belfry of Ivan the Great

The Belfry of Ivan the Great dominates the silhouette of the Moscow Kremlin. During the Middle Ages, the Church of John Climacus was located "under the bells," which had been erected in 1329 and later destroyed. The architect Bon Friazin was awarded the commission to build a two-story polygonal edifice containing a church on the ground floor in cooperation with Russian architects, and it was built from 1505 to 1508. The white stone for the socle and foundation came from Miachokovo near Moscow; the superstructure was constructed of oversized bricks.

The belfry acquired its present height and form under Tsar Boris Godunov in 1600. The huge gold letters on the triple frieze of the drum of the cupola name the builder and date of construction. Eighty-one meters high, the Belfry of Ivan the Great was the highest edifice of its time in Russia. It guaranteed security and served as an alarm tower and watchtower with a view extending for 25–30 kilometers.

Today, the slender tower rises in three octagonal blocks ringed by pilasters. Multi-tiered cornices with zigzag friezes on each octagonal element demarcate the top thirds, which are each comprised of a bell loft open on all sides with an arcade. The upper octagon is topped off by flame-shaped kokoshniks forming the transition to the cylindrical drum. At the foot of the dome shines a triple frieze with gold inscriptions.

▷ The soaring white body of the Belfry forms the compositional axis of the entire Kremlin ensemble. It integrates all of the Kremlin buildings, which vary greatly according to their date of origin, into a unified architectural complex and provides an urban accent for many miles around that commands the scene even in Moscow, a city of millions.

Master builder Petrok Maly (from Italy?) erected a low edifice with Renaissance ornamentation on the wide front facing the square next to "Ivan," which at that time had only two stories, as early as from 1532 to 1543. Experts disagree as to whether it was originally a Church of the Resurrection of Christ or a bell tower. The monumental belfry and the cupola apparently were added at the end of the 17th century. The cupola was designed in the Pskovian style and has double-banded columns. Previously, Patriarch Philaret had had another bell tower added on the north wall; this massive annex with corner turrets was thus named the Tower of Patriarch Philaret.

▽ Inscription beneath the dome of the Belfry: "By expression of the will of the Holy Trinity and by order of the great Tsar and Grand Prince Boris Feodorovich, Tsar of All Russia and Son of the Faithful High Tsar, Grand Prince Feodor Borissovich of All Russia, this church was built and gilded in the second year of their rule 108." The date refers to the time around 1600. The words illustrated below are *russi khram* ("of All Russia, this church...").

▷ The Tsar's Bell. The 800 *pud* of metal (one pud weighs 16.5 kilograms) needed to cast this bell came from an old, broken bell as well as from new metal. The Tsar's Bell weighs approximately 200 metric tons. The split-off piece on the pedestal weighs 11.5 metric tons alone; the bell measures 6.14 meters in height and 6.6 in diameter. The alloy consists of copper, tin, bronze, and other metals. This masterpiece is perfectly shaped. Palmettes, rosettes, and garlands are combined with medallions. The relief portraits of Tsar Alexei Michailovich and Empress Anna Ivanova are also magnificent. Inscriptions tell of the bell's origin.

The 21 bells that have decorated the belfry and its smaller partner up to the present are valuable for the history of Russian artistic casting. The largest among them, the 70-ton Uspenskii Bell, was cast by Ivan Savyalov in 1817–1819. Fires and wars shook the stability and solidity of the majestic belfry more than once. Before Napoleon's troops retreated from Moscow in 1812, they blew up the smaller belfry and the Tower of Patriarch Philaret. The small tower suffered severe damages, yet "Grand Ivan" only cracked.

Restoration activities have been underway since the 1970s. The metal cupola constructions, architectural details, and stuccowork were renovated, the roof was replaced, and the foundation of the small bell tower was stabilized. The cupolas were replated in gold. A hall for exhibitions was opened on the ground floor.

To the northwest lies the largest square in the Kremlin, Ivan Square. During the Middle Ages, the *prikazy* (state offices) were located around the square and every morning, the decrees and ordinances of the tsar were called out to the crowd. The civil servants had to announce the tsar's desires so that everyone could understand them; thus, they had to cry very loudly across Ivan Square. The saying "Cry Ivan" derives from this time.

A special attraction has been located near the Belfry for over two centuries: the Tsar's Bell. It was cast by Ivan Motorin and his son Michail Motorin with the assistance of numerous craftsmen from 1723 to 1735.

▷ View from the Grand Kremlin Palace over the domes of the Cathedral of the Annunciation toward Cathedral Square and the Belfry. To the left, the Uspenskii Cathedral; to the right, the Cathedral of the Archangel Michael.

140

▷ View of the Palace of Facets and the Tsar's Palace from Cathedral Square. Print made in 1856 of a drawing in the book *The Election and Coronation of Grand Prince Mikhail Feodorovich as Tsar*, published in 1672.

PALACES AND RESIDENCES

The Grand Kremlin Palace

In the southwest of the Kremlin stands the Grand Palace, an ensemble of secular and ecclesiastical buildings built over a period of five centuries, the incarnation of the best traditions in Russian architecture and the scene of numerous significant events in Russian history. Great plans were made in the 1770s for rebuilding the Grand Kremlin Palace, but they were thwarted by the political and financial difficulties of that period. The old palace designed by Bartolomeo Rastrelli (1733–1775) was not renovated until the eve of the 19th century, an age that was to bring turbulent, calamitous events. Chief among them was the war against Napoleon, the climax of which – the French occupation of Moscow and the Kremlin in 1812 – brought grave consequences to the city's monuments and palaces. Fires and natural catastrophes also did their part to harm the Grand Kremlin Palace. During the first quarter of the 19th century, the palace was now and then "polished up" superficially, usually for imperial visits to Moscow, a treatment which by no means sufficed. In 1836, a comprehensive program to renovate the old palace building was initiated under F. Richter, yet it soon became apparent that the old edifice no longer corresponded to the spirit of the times and the new conception of ideal beauty. The decision was made to build a new palace. A group of Russian architects – F. Richter, Nicholai Ivanovich Chishagov, P. Gerassimov, and V. Bakarev – took over construction of the new edifice under the direction of Konstantin Andreyevich Ton in 1838, and the building was completed in 1849.

Most of the older buildings that were incorporated into the new palace are located in the east and north sections, the more recent edifices in the south and west sections of the complex. A connecting passage on the west side links the Palace building to the somewhat more modest residence of the grand prince, next to which the Armory, a museum fitting in status for this palace, was later erected. After the mid-19th century the palace was commonly called the "Grand Kremlin Palace."

Pages 144/45: The Grand Kremlin Palace as seen from the southwest. This mighty complex on Borovitskii Hill is an incredibly intricate ensemble of secular and ecclesiastical buildings erected during and after the 15th century. The massive 19th century wings dominate its appearance.

▷ △ View of the Kremlin between the stone bridge and the living bridge [Pontos Bridge] from the far bank of the Moskva. 18th century, Historical Museum.

▷ ▽ Ground plan of the first floor of the Grand Kremlin Palace (taken from "Le Grand Palais du Kremlin, Guide du visiteur," Moscow 1912). 1. Parade Staircase; 2. Antechamber; 3. St. George Hall; 4. St. Alexander Hall; 5. St. Andrew Hall; 6. Hall of the Chevaliers Guards; 7. St. Catherine Hall; 8. State Drawing Room; 9. State Bedroom; 10. Church of the Birth of Mary; 11. Winter Garden; 12. Residential wing; 13. Golden Tsaritsa Chamber; 14. Holy Vestibule; 15. Palace of Facets; 16. St. Vladimir Hall; 17. Cathedral of the Annunciation; 18. Church of St. Catherine; 19. Church of the Repository of the Robe; 20. Amusement Palace; 21. Barracks of the Chevaliers Guards; 22. Barracks of the Officers; 23. Boyars Square; 24. Terem Palace; 25. Church of the Savior in the Forest; 26. Stables; 27. Private Apartments; 28. Armory.

146

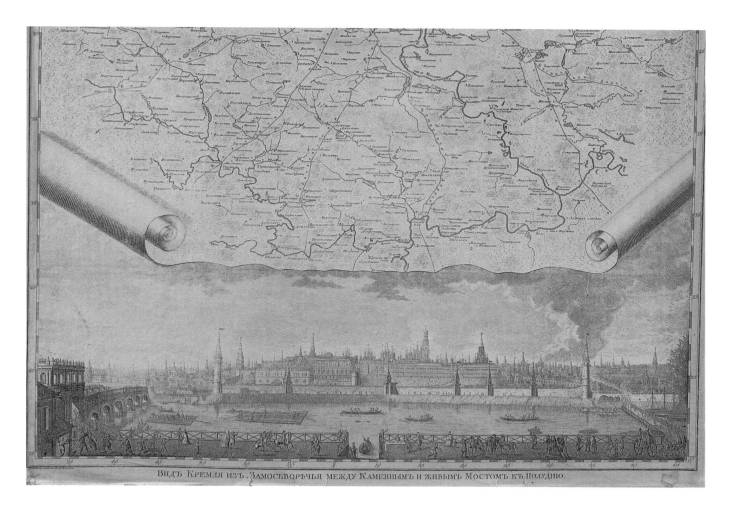

ВИДЪ КРЕМЛЯ ИЗЪ ЗАМОСКВОРѢЧЬЯ МЕЖДУ КАМЕННЫМЪ И ЖИВЫМЪ МОСТОМЪ КЪ ПОЛУДНЮ.

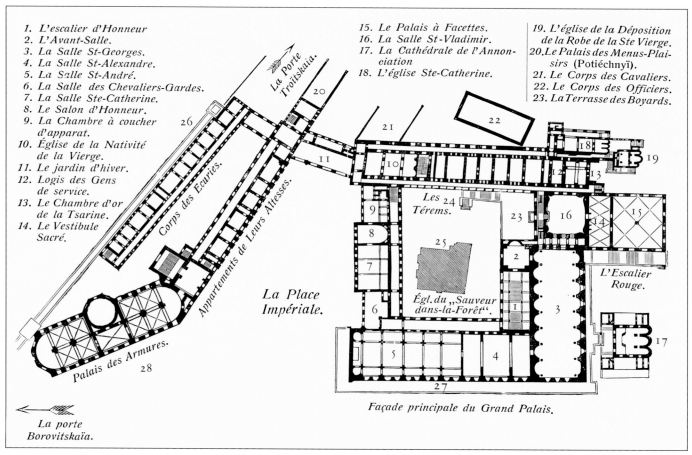

1. L'escalier d'Honneur
2. L'Avant-Salle.
3. La Salle St-Georges.
4. La Salle St-Alexandre.
5. La Salle St-André.
6. La Salle des Chevaliers-Gardes.
7. La Salle Ste-Catherine.
8. Le Salon d'Honneur.
9. La Chambre à coucher d'apparat.
10. Église de la Nativité de la Vierge.
11. Le jardin d'hiver.
12. Logis des Gens de service.
13. Le Chambre d'or de la Tsarine.
14. Le Vestibule Sacré.

15. Le Palais à Facettes.
16. La Salle St-Vladimir.
17. La Cathédrale de l'Annonciation
18. L'église Ste-Catherine.

19. L'église de la Déposition de la Robe de la Ste Vierge.
20. Le Palais des Menus-Plaisirs (Potiéchnyï).
21. Le Corps des Cavaliers.
22. Le Corps des Officiers.
23. La Terrasse des Boyards.

La Porte Troïtskaia.

Corps des Écuries.

Appartements de Leurs Altesses.

La Place Impériale.

Palais des Armures.

La porte Borovitskaïa.

Les Térems.

Égl. du „Sauveur dans-la-Forêt".

L'Escalier Rouge.

Façade principale du Grand Palais.

Older residences in the Grand Kremlin Palace

The old tsar's residence was integrated into the new structure during construction of the Grand Kremlin Palace (1838–1849). According to the Kremlin tradition, great attention was paid to harmoniously blending the old with the new, eclectic building styles.

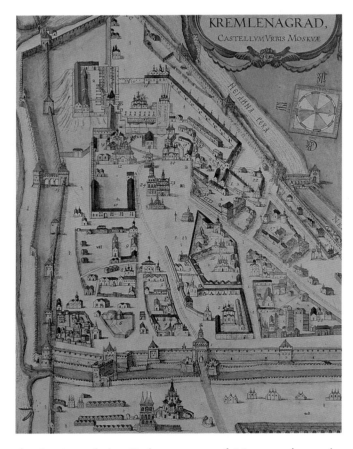

△ Section of the Godunov map of Moscow drawn in 1597. This document shows the old residence buildings in partial relief (ground plans with partially projected façades). Easily distinguishable are the cubical Palace of Facets and the floor plan of the building that formerly stood where Terem Palace is now located.

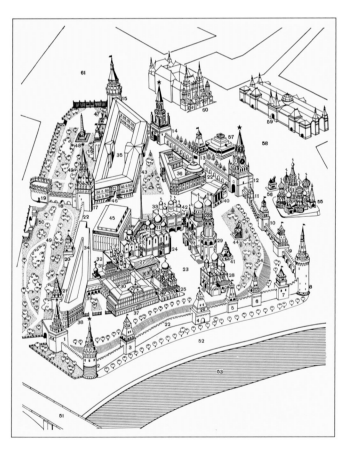

△ Bird's-eye view of the present-day Kremlin. Number 27 (Palace of Facets) and number 30 (Terem Palace) denote the most important existing parts of older residences in the Grand Kremlin Palace.

▷ Section of the façade decorations created in 1636 on Terem Palace.

The Palace of Facets and the Holy Vestibule

On the west side of the square between Uspenskii and Blagoveshchenskii Cathedrals stands the famous Palace of Facets. The white faceted limestone covering its east facade rustications probably gave the building its name. Built from 1487 to 1491 by the Italian architects Marco Ruffo and Pietro Antonio Solario, the Palace of Facets is considered the oldest existing secular building in Moscow. The low cross-vault roof of the nearly square chamber rests on a single central pier, which lends the room an effect of spaciousness. Daylight falls through tall, wide windows into this majestic hall from three sides. In the evening, the hall is lit by four massive chandeliers made in the 19th century of dark bronze and modeled on Novgorod prototypes.

The interior decorations of the ceremonious hall have been changed several times. The first murals dated from the end of the 16th century. They depicted religious themes, fables, historical events, scenes of daily life, and portraits of grand princes. Their philosophical and historical dimensions contributed to an ambiguity typical of Old Russian painting.

Fires damaged the Palace of Facets so badly that a renovation became necessary as early as the 1660s. The Muscovite icon painter Simon Ushakov was commissioned to reproduce the frescos. Before he started work in 1668, he prepared a comprehensive description of all pictures. At the end of the 17th century, during Peter I's reign, the walls were whitewashed and covered with raspberry-colored brocade on which the state eagles were embroidered in silver. In 1882, the Beloussov brothers from Palekh repainted the hall according to Ushakov's descriptions. At the same time, the plaster reliefs on the central pier dating from the 18th century were replaced by paintings. The palace facade was changed considerably in 1684–1685 when Ossip Startsev redid the windows during renovation of the hall. Splendid architraves supported by columns richly decorated with stone carvings were added to the windows. At approximately the same time, the roof was covered with gilt and painted tin.

△ The Palace of Facets is probably both one of the most important and peculiar monuments to Russian architecture. It also reflects the opening of the country to Western Europe. The architectural forms of the Renaissance have retained elements of the Late Gothic style, such as the cubical shape, the almost completely unsegmented façades, the simple cornice shapes, the closely spaced double windows, and the slender spiral columns on their edges. In the 17th century, the windows where widened and their columns removed. The older windows have been preserved only on the side walls.

The Chamber of Facets was the largest audience and throne room in the Kremlin. Here, foreign emissaries were received, decisions important for the fate of the Russian nation made, and meetings of the national assemblies held. Ivan the Terrible celebrated the conquest of Kazan and Peter I his victory over the Swedish at Poltava in this hall. On ceremonious occasions the State Hall appeared especially festive: the floor was covered with Persian carpets, valuable fabrics with gold embroideries hung on the benches and shutters, and numerous costly vessels shone on the tables. However, the focus of the room was formed by the shelves around the rectangular pier, which held many showpieces of silver and gold. Many of them, enthusiastically described by contemporaries and chroniclers, can now be seen in the Armory.

The Palace of Facets has also been the scene of important events in our times: until recently, the Senior Council of the Supreme Soviet of the USSR met here. Today, large receptions are held in this chamber during popular and national holidays.

Soviet art historians and restorers carefully maintain the original decoration inside the Facet Chamber. In 1949, restorers from Palekh cleaned the layers of dirt from the wall paintings. In 1954, the newer layers of paint were removed from the facade; subsequently, its initial state was reproduced (with the exception of the socle, which also used to be faceted). On the whole, the buildings' original appearance has been preserved quite well despite the various changes made over the centuries.

Pages 152/53: The Chamber of Facets is a huge, light hall with an area of 495 square meters. The vault measures approximately 9 meters at its crown. The chamber is completely covered with paintings portraying the Days of Creation, Paradise, and the Expulsion of the First Parents on the cross vaults; next to the tsar's palace, the Dream of the Prophet Daniel and Jacob's Ladder; Moses's Burning Bush on the south wall; the First Fathers, evangelists, and prophets on the bases of the vaults; the Life of Joseph on the north and west walls; near the crown, Moses in front of the Ark of the Covenant, David being admonished by the Prophet Nathan, and Solomon in the Temple. Near the Tsar's throne are also scenes from Russian history. To the right of the entrance in the crown of the blind arch is the secret window, through which tsaritsas and daughters of tsars could observe the ceremonies that they were not allowed to attend.

▷ On the window splays and two panels of the east and south walls, Russian princes and tsars are portrayed as personifications of Russian history. The founder of the Russian state, Grand Prince Riurik, Grand Prince Igor, and Grand Prince Svyatoslav Igoryevich III are recognizable in the lower picture. The upper picture portrays Grand Prince Fzyevolod with his sons.

The Palace of Facets was included in the new spurt of restorations in 1968. The central pier was stabilized with metal constructions, and its reliefs were recreated on a red background and covered with a new layer of gold. Even the pillars of the 15th-century portal were cared for: the stuccowork and layers of paint were protected and regilding was carried out.

In centuries past, the Red Staircase led to the Palace of Facets, was connected with the Holy Vestibule, and served as a gala entryway. The present appearance of the Holy Vestibule dates from the 1840s, when the Palace of Facets and its surroundings were incorporated into the Grand Kremlin Palace. Two new doors were added to the two original white ones and connected the Holy Vestibule to St. Vladimir Hall. Because the old frescos had fallen victim to time, F. Zavjalov painted the walls in 1849 with Biblical motifs and themes from Russian history ("Sergius of Radonesh blesses Prince Dmitrii Donskoy before battle with the Tatars" and "Prince Vladimir of Kiev converts to Christianity"). These paintings were restored in 1968.

▷ △ The Holy Vestibule, unchanged since having been decorated in 1838–1849. The photograph shows the two new doors that connect the Holy Vestibule with St. Vladimir Hall. Part of mural painted by F. Zavyalov can be seen at the left. Gilt chandeliers and wall lamps have illuminated the Holy Vestibule since the 19th century.

▷ Gilt inscriptions above the foundation stone of the Holy Vestibule.

The Golden Tsaritsa Chamber

Another valuable architectural monument dates from the 16th century: the Golden Tsaritsa Chamber, erected for Irina Godunova, the wife of Feodor Ivanovich. This small, rectangular palace was built on a closed arcade foundation at the east end of Terem Palace. Its projecting molding, colorful ornamentation, and doorway decorated with filigree work bear traces of the Italian Renaissance. When the Upper Church of the Savior was erected atop the chamber in the 17th century, stone arches and metal supports were installed inside the room.

The chronicles report that the Tsaritsa Chamber was adorned with fantastically beautiful murals on golden backgrounds that were renovated several times in the 17th and 18th centuries, the last time on the occasion of the crowning of Paul I (in 1797). Legendary events from the lives of famous tsaritsas and princesses served as motifs: the Byzantine Empresses Helena, Irina, and Theodora, the Georgian ruler Tamara, and the Russian Princess Olga. An informative inscription accompanied each picture. Particularly impressive are the imaginative compositions of the pictures and their brilliant range of colors, which in combination convey a faithful picture of the reception hall of the Russian tsaritsas. In 1589, Tsaritsa Irina received the Greek Metropolitan Arsenius, who had come to Moscow for the installation of an independent patriarchal see in Russia and was the first foreigner allowed to view the chambers of the Russian tsaritsas. He described this chamber "full of light and gold," telling of his boundless admiration: "Costly paintings gleamed on the wall, jewels of inestimable value glittered in the golden icon frames, silk carpets from Persia embroidered with gold shimmered under one's feet, valuable vessels and goblets stood so close together that one could not even guess at their number." Thanks to the Kremlin restorers, the original, 16th-century paintings were saved in restorations of 1925, 1947, and the 1970s.

Since the 1840s, the Golden Tsaritsa Chamber and the Guards Room – a room for the palace guards which led to other chambers – have been part of the Grand Kremlin Palace. The 16th-century Golden Doorway with its intricate Renaissance ornamentations and two windows have been preserved. Also still in existence are the 17th-century portal and the white stone encasing on the window of the Guards Room. Konstantin Andreyevich Ton artistically employed the stone encasing in an arch-shaped recess in Vladimir Hall.

▷ Doorway between the living quarters and the Tsaritsa Chamber. A painting of the Mother of God dating from the 17th century is visible through the doorway in the Tsaritsa Chamber.

△ The Golden Tsaritsa Chamber was decorated with frescos in the 16th century, their golden backgrounds giving the room its name. The paintings portray episodes from the lives of tsars, grand princesses, and Byzantine empresses (Helena, Theodora, Irina, and others), deeds of the legendary Georgian ruler Tamara, and the Russian Princess Olga. The detailed depictions of daily events are a special feature of these paintings (for example, the baptism of Princess Olga, her journey to Byzantium, her refusal of the emperor's proposal of marriage, and her return to Kiev are portrayed at length). All of the paintings have captions. The segment shown here depicts the arrival of Prince Dmitrii Zolunski after his victory over the potentate Batu. He is carrying the head of the loser impaled on his spear. The painting, by an unknown artist, dates from the 16th century.

△ Colored, rosette-shaped window with lead glazing. View toward the Belfry on Cathedral Square.

△ Inside the Golden Tsaritsa Chamber.

Terem Palace

Terem Palace, the oldest part of the tsar's residence, forms the north front of the Grand Kremlin Palace together with some side buildings. Its name derives from the old Russian word for a luxurious dwelling.

At the request of Mikhail Feodorovich, Bashen Ogurtsov, Trefil Sharutin, Antip Konstantinov, and Larion Ushakov in 1635–1636 built two additional floors onto the two stories dating from the 16th century. The centuries-old tradition of Russian timber construction was applied in a fascinating manner to Terem Palace, even though this huge edifice was made of white stone. Inside and out, it was embellished with all conceivable types of magnificence known at the time: white stone carvings; colorful tiles; wrought-iron roofs; brilliant frescos; plant motifs originally painted in bright colors; window linings and portals; luxuriant acanthus ornamentation on the vaults, pillars and supports; portrayals of animals; and leaf masks. To emphasize wealth, great quantities of gold paint were applied to the wall paintings. According to chronicles from that period, the roofs and gutters also were painted and gilded: A rarity in those days were the colorful isinglass windowpanes that allowed the sunbeams to play fancifully on the colorful tiles and splendid carpets.

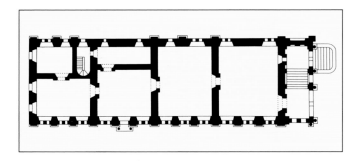

△ Ground plan of the Terem Palace "state floor" in Moscow.

▷ Terem Palace rises in an unusual manner. Its attic, the actual *terem*, originally served as a resting place and a bedroom. Later, the name was applied to the entire structure. The original terem was located on the fifth floor. The bottom two stories (the cellar and the gallery) are the remains of a 16th-century palace; the upper stories date chiefly from the 17th century. The building is shaped so that one story seemingly grows out of another. The forecourts formerly served as promenades. In the 19th century, Konstantin Andreyevich Thon redesigned the lower stories and encased their façades. Inside he created small rooms for workshops, servants, and ladies in waiting. The upper stories' façades date from 1635–1636. A new conception of the function of windows in Russian architecture is illustrated by their shapes; no longer were they considered mere necessities, but were seen as an architectural form and embellished.

◁ Double arch with a hanging keystone in the shape of an animal's head (a lion with a golden apple in his mouth as a symbol of discretion).

▷ The Golden Stairway in Terem Palace. It leads to the Upper Platform of the Savior, which links Terem Palace with the Upper Cathedral of the Savior. The stairway's name is probably derived from the magnificent paintings around it, which are adorned with quantities of gold. The basic structure of this small element is built of white limestone adorned with carvings. A pair of lions bearing shields sit on the pedestals at the foot of the stairs.

The square rooms with low, vaulted roofs in the existing part of the fourth floor used to be the private quarters of the tsars. The first one was called the Dining Chamber (or Front Room). In the mornings, boyars – the Russian nobility – waited for the Sovereign over All Russia to present him their petitions and requests. In the next room, the Chamber of the Cross (also called the Meditation Chamber), "sittings" of the tsar with the nobility took place. Behind this is the Throne Room, the actual working room, in which the tsars sometimes also dined in the circle of their closest friends. In 1660, Patriarch Nikon was sentenced by the Council Tribunal of the Russian Orthodox Church in the Throne Room. Because he had tried to place the authority of the church above that of the tsar, Nikon was stripped of his duties and honors as patriarch. The Throne Room is probably the most elegant chamber in Terem Palace. Gilt heraldic devices from all parts of Russia decorate its purplish-red walls. The tsar's throne, covered with brocade, stands in the middle of the room.

The fourth and last in this suite of rooms is the Bedchamber, in its middle a canopied wooden bed with carvings. Next door is the Prayer Room, with two gilt iconostases – including works from the 17th and 18th centuries – and a tiled stove. The fourth floor of the palace also houses the spacious nursery, which is surrounded by an open terrace.

Wars and natural catastrophes took their toll an Terem Palace; the French occupation of Moscow in 1812 had especially disastrous consequences. Not until the 1830s and 40s did F. Richter reproduce the interior decorations of individual rooms according to drawings by Feodor Grigoryevich Zolntsev. Oak windowsills and furniture were reproduced, careful attention being paid to creating them in strict accordance with the 17th-century tradition of woodcutting. However, these restorations are sure to have altered the original appearance of the building considerably.

△ The Duma room (the meeting room of the boyar parliament). In this room, matters of state were conducted and, above all, many conflicts between boyars were settled. The 17th-century table is carved and gilt; its tabletop is painted. The Mother of God and Child on a crescent moon are painted on the ceiling. The ornamentation is in the Old Russian style.

△ The best-preserved rooms in Terem Palace are those on the fourth floor, which formerly were reserved for the tsar. They are almost all the same size and their windows face south. Five rooms in all lie in a row on this floor. However, because the doors are not lined up precisely on one axis, the suite does not have the typical passage-like character. The room shown here is the antechamber, where the boyars closest to the tsar gathered early every morning to greet him. Sometimes the chamber was also used for small festive occasions, for which tables were set up.

▷ Stairs to the fifth floor of the terem, the *teremok* (small terem for the children). The floors and rooms of the terem are connected by several stairways. Carved stone ornamentation, wood carvings, and unusually colorful tiles with flower motifs blend in an extremely picturesque ensemble. The windows contain tinted isinglass.

△ The tsaritsa's bedchamber. In the middle stands a wooden fourposter bed with canopy and carvings. The present wall paintings were created in 1836–1838 by T. Kissilov according to drawings by the scholar Feodor Grigoryevich Zolntsev. Most of the decorations consist of oil paintings of plant motifs and on some religious themes. Fragments of the paintings from the late 17th century still exist.

▷ Almost every room in Terem Palace has its own tiled stove, the background color of which differs in each room so that it corresponds to the chambers' dominant colors.

Soviet experts are carefully examining and painstakingly restoring the Kremlin monuments even today. Sergei Timofeyevich Konenkov, a well-known Soviet sculptor belonging to the older generation, wrote in his memoirs: "... Since the first days of the new rule – as early as November 1917 – the old Moscow Kremlin has been a focus of the cultural revolution." The first discovery was made in 1919, when restorers found a fragment of an extremely elegant Renaissance cornice on the east facade of the Golden Tsaritsa Chamber. In the 1920s, further finds were made: old frescos in the Terem Palace Dining Hall and several stone buildings from the 14th century, including the Church of the Raising of Lazarus, were discovered. In the 1950s, attempts were made to remove more recent layers of paint from murals in Terem Palace and from the Golden Staircase. During the process, paintings from 1680 were uncovered in the Upper Cathedral of the Savior.

Archaeological and architectonic studies carried out during construction of the Palace of Congress in the Kremlin (1959–1961) provided valuable information for the restoration of Terem Palace during the 1970s and '80s.

In 1968, the original guise of the Palace's three upper floors could be restored: their colorfully painted windows, which contrast attractively with the bright red walls, and the interior decoration of many *terem* chambers.

Pages 172/73: The Golden Room, formerly simply called "The Room." It was one of the tsar's offices, and only those closest to him were allowed entrance in the 17th century. Occasionally, the tsar would listen to a church service here, and he had beggars and prisoners fed in the room as a token of his charity. The middle window was also called the Petitioners' Window. A box was lowered from it to the courtyard below so that anyone could place his petition to the tsar in it. The saying "put it in the long box" is a reminder of this custom. This chamber, completely covered in red, has a luxurious gold decor, for which it was named the Golden Room under Tsar Mikhail Feodorovich. The Savior seated on a throne and surrounded by saints is painted on the ceiling. Between the saints and on the window reveals, coats of arms from various Russian regions are portrayed. A chair now stands where the tsar's throne, presently kept in the Armory, once was located. The book about the election of Mikhail Feodorovich as tsar (from 1672, now in the Armory) used to lie open on the table in front of the middle window.

▷ Portal in the fifth floor leading to the teremok. Above the entrance, there was once an inscription engraved in stone proclaiming that Tsar Mikhail Feodorovich had this teremok built for his offspring, his sons Alexei and Ivan, in 1637. A platform, called the Upper Stone Courtyard in the 17th century, surrounds the teremok. The portal and frieze of the teremok are decorated with fantastic reliefs showing exotic plants and animals: squirrels, parrots, lions, fairy-tale animals such as unicorns and winged griffons and mythological figures such as satyrs and archers. On the crown of the door's arch is the popular symbolic pelican that tears the flesh from its breast to feed its young. The mixture of grotesque and didactic elements is typical for this period of Russian art.

Older Churches in the Grand Kremlin Palace

Part of the task facing Ton in building the Grand Kremlin Palace was the integration of older ecclesiastical buildings into the new edifice, such as the Church of the Raising of Lazarus, the Church of the Birth of Mary, St. Catherine's Church, the Upper Church of the Savior, the Church of the Resurrection, and the Church of the Crucifixion. Most of them had already undergone many rebuildings and alterations, destructions, and renovations in their eventful histories.

△ Section of the Godunov map from 1597. The segment pictured above shows the area where the Grand Kremlin Palace now stands.

△ Section of a modern sketch from a bird's-eye view. The older church structures are located under the numerous domes at number 32 (the Terem churches) and under the single dome at number 31 (the Churches of the Resurrection of Lazarus and the Birth of Mary).

▷ View from the copiously decorated cupolas of the Terem churches, now located at the northeast corner of the Grand Kremlin Palace, towards the Belfry of Ivan the Great.

The Churches of the Raising of Lazarus and the Birth of Mary

The Church of the Raising of Lazarus is situated on the ground floor at the western end of Terem Palace. This compact stone building was erected in 1393 to replace a wooden Lazarus church at the order of Princess Yevdokina, the widow of Dmitrii Donskoy, who had won the Battle of Kulikovo. Because the battle had taken place on the day of Mary's birth in 1380, the church was dedicated to this order. The chronicles report that Theophanos the Greek, Zemyon Chorni, and their pupils painted the inside of the new building in 1395. The church suffered heavy damages several times in the 15th century. In 1514, Alovisio Novo erected a new brick vault and added a second, five-domed church on top of it, to which the old patronage of the Birth of Mary was transferred. The stone crypt below, which was then named the "Auxiliary Altar of the Raising of Lazarus," was walled off and forgotten. It reemerged during construction of the Grand Kremlin Palace and was renovated. Further restorations were carried out from 1923 to 1928 and 1949 to 1952.

The superstructure, subsequently called the Church of the Birth of Mary, was expanded from 1681 to 1685 and another church room added on top, which, however, was torn down shortly thereafter and replaced by the single-domed roof of the present church.

▷ Church of the Raising of Lazarus. View of one of the mighty, round limestone monolith piers. This structure, built in the 14th century of white ashlars, is the oldest existing church in the Kremlin. The room has striking proportions and massive elements; the ogee-arched niche with its fat circular molding is typical of this style.

△ Church of the Birth of Mary. View from the porch through the portal archs to the iconostasis. The rooms were redecorated during construction of the Grand Kremlin Palace and have since remained unchanged. The splendid, painted masonry on the entryways dates from the 17th century, as do most of the pictures in the iconostasis, whereas the resplendent gold paintings between the portals and the starred firmament are 19th-century works.

▷ Church of the Birth of Mary. The icon "The Birth of Mary" is depicted in the first row of the iconostasis, second to the right of the Tsar's Door. It was made in a Moscow workshop in the 17th century. This place is usually reserved for the icon the church was built to honor. A series of smaller pictures portraying the life of the Mother of God surround the central picture of her birth, which also depicts drinking swans as symbols of purity. The splendid interconnected buildings and utensils of daily life are particulary expressive and beautiful in this picture.

St. Catherine's Church

The architect John Taler built this church in 1627. It is part of the group of private churches on the east side of Terem Palace adjacent to the northern wall of the Golden Tsaritsa Chamber on the second floor. In the Middle Ages it was the main church in the women's half of the palace, but by the 17th century it stood in the midst of numerous additions.

The interior of St. Catherine's Church was completely changed in the middle of the 19th century. The alterations and redecorations were carried out according to plans made by Konstantin Andreyevich Ton, and academician Feodor Grigoreyevich Zolntsev played a prominent part in their execution. Soviet restorers have recreated the original architectural form and also restored, among other elements, the old gallery passage and the stairs on the north side of the church. The Church of the Resurrection of the Holy Lord of Praise is located above St. Catherine's Church.

△ Interior of St. Catherine's Church after the restoration
in the 1960s. Iconostasis from the 19th century.

The Upper Cathedral of the Savior

The Upper Cathedral of the Savior adjoins St. Catherine's Church and the Landing with the Golden Grille at the easternmost part of Terem Palace. Built by the architects of Terem Palace in 1635–1636, it served as the private chapel of the Russian tsars. It was united under one roof with the Church of the Holy Lord of Praise and the Church of the Crucifixion by Ossip Startsev in 1681, which led to their commonly being called the "Upper Churches in front of the Tsar's Door." Instead of building 15 cupolas above three churches, as was typical of the Orthodox style, Startsev had only 11 erected and placed them along the rectangular outline in the east part of Terem Palace. The rather small cupolas are very graceful and their gilt openwork crosses catch the eye of the beholder. The brick drums of the cupolas and the cornices of the roof have majolica tile decorations with luxuriant scroll motifs. This superior craftmanship dates from the second half of the 17th century. It is said that well-known masters such as Ignat Maximov, Stepan Ivanov, and the potter Ippolit the Elder participated in their production.

Especially noteworthy among the 17th century icons are those by Feodor Zubov. The engraved silver iconostasis in the Upper Cathedral of the Savior dates from the 18th century. During restorations in 1949, fragments of pictures from the 17th century were discovered on the vaults under the 19th-century murals. The Cathedral also bore a second name, "Savior Behind the Golden Grille," because it is separated from the landing of the same name by a colorfully painted and gilt iron grille in which enchanting fairy-tale animals and grotesque faces of a rare beauty play among its spiral bars.

△ The principal attraction in the main room of the Upper Cathedral of the Savior is the Tsar's Door. Whereas most of the icons date from the second half of the 17th century, the greater part of the upper addition is in the late Baroque style of the 18th century. The Tsar's Door was built in 1778. It is covered with very finely engraved silver reliefs (above left, the Washing of Feet; above right, the Trinity; on the wings of the doors, the Annunciation).

△ The portal between St. Catherine's Church and the Upper Cathedral of the Savior. The entrance to the cathedral is on a level with the Golden Stairway and is closed off by a golden grille. According to legend, this grille was cast in 1670 of copper coins removed from circulation after the Copper Revolt. Actually, the grille is made of wrought iron and gilt and is covered with metallic luster (colored enamel on a gold or silver base). The intricate pattern is an excellent example of 17th-century Muscovite goldsmithery.

◁ The Longinus icon in the Upper Cathedral of the Savior. According to legend, Longinus was the Roman centurion who commanded the soldiers at the Crucifixion of Jesus on Golgotha and later died as a Christian martyr. This icon dates from the 1670s and resembles Simon Ushakov's work. It was probably painted by Tichon Filyatev, an icon painter in the Armory commissioned by the court; another opinion claims it was created by Feodor Zubov. The panel covered with silver sheet displays a method of painting new for that time in which the inner figure was shaded. The coloring is not as luminous and transparent as that of Ushakov's work, but the figure shows a more animated facial expression and gestures.

▷ Inner hallway designed by Konstantin Andreyevich Thon on the outer northern wall of St. Catherine's Church.

The Church of the Resurrection

The Church of the Resurrection – also called the Church of the Glorified Resurrection or the Church of the Holy Lord of Praise – adjoins the Upper Cathedral of the Savior on the same floor. The ceremonious, brightly colored decorations in its interior are striking and include such excellent works of art as the iconostasis and the choir with its gilt Baroque carvings from the second half of the 17th century. Heavy clusters of grapes, full acanthus leaves, and winding scroll-and-leaf patterns cover the returned moldings on the columns and entablatures. Most of the icons are from the same period as the top part of the iconostasis and reveal the hand of the master Pospyelev. Their coloring, designed to catch the effects of light and shadow, presages the realistic Russian secular painting of the 18th century.

◁ Multi-armed chandelier of gilt silver. It was a gift from the King Carl XI of Sweden to Tsar Alexei Feodorovich, the father of Peter I. The five foolish and five prudent virgins depicted on the volutes are made of embossed silver and cast metal. The individually designed robes and the expert characterization of the figures mark this outstanding work from Germany.

△ Iconostasis in the Church of the Resurrection.

The Church of the Crucifixion

One floor above the Upper Cathedral of the Savior is the Church of the Crucifixion, built in 1681. It is famous for its iconostasis, whose icons are made of a harmonious blend of silk fabrics; only the hands and faces of the figures have been painted. The iconostasis is considered to be the joint production of the Armory painters Ivan Bezmin, Vassili Poznanski, and Bogdan Zaltanov. Poznanski, who had emigrated from Polish Poznang when he was only twelve, probably directed the project.

△ Two oval icons with silk appliqués in the iconostasis of the Church of the Resurrection.

△ Icon of Mary with the Seven Swords of Sorrow.

19th- and 20th-Century Sections of the Grand Kremlin Palace

Lofty and majestic, the Moscow residence of the tsars dominates the southern part of the Kremlin. The palace silhouette is impressively and distinctly unassuming. The basement of the building's front, which faces the Moskva, forms a powerful basis above which the main floor and its high windows rise. The socle is encased in gray stone quarried in Tatarovo (near Moscow).

The hipped roof ends in a gilt balustrade with a flagpole, on which the national flag is flown on holidays. Five ogee-shaped archivolts form a unit on the roof that displays the Soviet coat of arms and the Cyrillic letters "CCCP" (Russian abbreviation for the Union of Soviet Socialist Republics).

Konstantin Andreyevich Ton strove to apply the newest developments in the engineering of his time to the construction of the largest palace in the Kremlin during the first third of the 19th century. The pig-iron trusses supporting the roof were a technical novelty, as were metal ceiling structures, the use of cement, sheets of pig iron on the floors, hollow columns of zinc, suspended roofs, and hot-air heating.

On both sides of the rather simple state entrance, white marble slabs with the gold inscriptions "The Supreme Soviet of the USSR" and "The Supreme Soviet of the Russian Soviet Federated Socialist Republic" attest that the seats of the parliaments of the Soviet Union and the largest republic in the USSR are located here.

Pages 192/93: The gilt domes of the Kremlin Churches on Cathedral Square. On the left, the Cathedral of the Assumption; behind it, the Belfry of Ivan the Great; on the right, the particularly graceful domes of the Terem churches; behind them, the Cathedral of the Archangel.

▷ △ View of the main wing of the Grand Kremlin Palace from the Moskva.

▷ The Moscow Kremlin in 1971. Pen-and-ink drawing by Alexei Hamtsov. This section of the panorama shows the monumental Grand Kremlin Palace complex in the middle and behind it, the modern Palace of Congress.

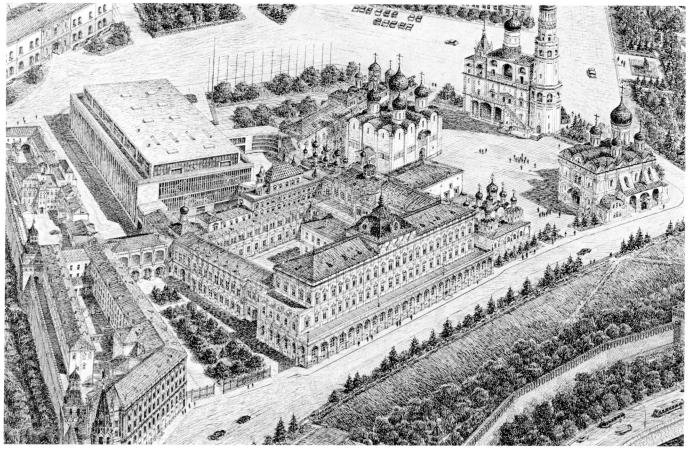

From the State Parade Antechamber with its four mighty, dark-gray granite columns, one enters the left wing of the bottom floor, on which is located the Private Apartments, a private, seven-room suite for the tsar's family. A festive white stairway leads to the State Parade Chambers on the second floor.

An exit on the middle landing of the marble staircase leads to Cathedral Square. The pointed arch of the Parade Stairway rests on ten marble piers connected by bronze grilles. Behind them extend two galleries; in the one on the right hangs a painting by Adolphe Yvon portraying the decisive moment in the battle against the Tatars on Kulikovo Field in 1380, a significant fight in Russian history. The three-meter-high crystal vases on either side of the entrance to the vestibule, with their gilt bronze edges, are noteworthy. The door to the vestibule is a masterpiece of 19th-century Russian carpentry – five meters high and made of wood from nut trees without using a single nail or glue. A chain of halls named for old Russian orders lies behind this door: St. George, St. Vladimir, St. Catherine, St. Andrew, and St. Alexander Halls.

The Grand Kremlin Palace overshadows all other Western European palaces of that period in terms of size and ornateness. Colorful types of highly decorative stones from the Urals were used here: malachite, granite, and several sorts of jasper. The diverse stone adornments are augmented by manifold stucco ornaments, artistic carvings and inlays of valuable woods, mother-of-pearl and tortoise-shell products, porcelain and bronze decorations, a unique collection of clocks, and splendid chandeliers that, alone and in combination, realistically and comprehensively reflect the 19th-century conceptions of beauty and style. It can be added here that pieces of furniture, decorations, and textiles were usually prepared for the Kremlin Palace on special commission and in only one issue by manufacturers in St. Petersburg and Moscow.

▷ △ Painting of a battle, which hangs at the upper end of the Parade Stairway. This painting by Adolphe Yvon depicts the Battle of Kulikovo on September 8, 1380, one of the most dramatic moments in the history of the Russian state's resistance to the Mongol-Tatar yoke. It was probably painted in 1850. The hero swinging his saber in the middle of the scene is Prince Dmitrii Donskoy, who succeeded in sending the Hordes of Khan Mamai to flight; he was given the surname Donskoy in honor of his victory on a battlefield on the Don River.

▷ The Parade Stairway. The flat roof of the Parade Hall is supported by four monoliths of Zerdov granite with Doric capitals and bases of white Carrara marble. Eight pilasters made of the same granite stand opposite the monoliths, as do four corner pilasters. The walls are of artificial marble. Massive bronze lamps have been placed next to each monolith. The floors are covered with sheets of gray stone from Tallin. At the upper end of the stairs hangs the painting of Lenin's appearance at the third Komsomol Congress (in 1922), created by a group of painters under the direction of B.W. Johanson in 1950.

196

St. Vladimir Hall

The two halls of state, St. Vladimir Hall and St. George Hall, are located in the huge east wing of the Grand Kremlin Palace. St. Vladimir Hall has an octagonal ground plan with alternating narrow and wide sides. Arch motifs dominate its walls: the wide sides each have an arcade with three round arches, the middle one of which opens onto a passage; the narrow walls each have a round-arched niche. A completely regular, triforium-like gallery with three round arches per axis extends around the hall above the sixteen axes of the octagon. The powerful cupola rises to a height of approximately 18 meters above the gallery. Its rhomboid-shaped segments seem to lean towards the circular, six-meter-high lantern. Each roof segment is covered with stuccowork in scroll-and-leaf patterns that surround medallions depicting the insignia of the Order of St. Vladimir. The decor, comprised of different types of marble and stucco with gold reliefs on the profiles and ornaments, is markedly eclectic and hovers between the Baroque and Classic styles. Pieces of wood from nut trees and stained oak have been laid in diverse symmetrical patterns in the parquet floors. A bronze chandelier weighing 1,700 kilograms and bearing 200 candle-shaped lamps on three tiers hangs in the center of the room.

▷ View of St. Vladimir Hall, which is located between the older palace structures and St. George Hall in the northeast corner of the Grand Kremlin Palace. It occupies part of the former boyar square, where the tsar's subjects waited outdoors for him to appear. Today, ceremonies take place in St. Vladimir Hall when international treaties and agreements are signed and distinctions are awarded by the government.

St. George Hall

The largest and most festive hall in the Grand Kremlin Palace was named for the Order of St. George, which was founded in 1769. Its dimensions are gigantic: 61 meters long, 20.5 meters wide, and 17 meters high at the crown. A tremendous polygonal cloister vault rises above the elongated hall and is supported by seven pairs of wall pillars. The extravagant stucco decor lends the structure an additional sense of heaviness. The reinforcing arches, "overgrown" with plant ornamentation, divide the barrel and connect the wall pillars. Rosettes depicting large flowers have been placed in the coffers, and the vault caps are covered with lively thickets of flowers and vines.

Peter Karlovich Klodt has plastered two identical stucco reliefs of the victorious St. George on the south and north fronts. The hollow zinc columns are unusual: they are placed in front of the piers and have plaster Corinthian capitals in the Classic style and a spiral decor of oak garlands. Personifications of the tsardoms stand on high pedestals above the broad returned molding: robed female figures of a cool beauty and in classic poses, created by the sculptor Ivan Petrovich Vitali. Marble slabs bearing the names of the knights of the order have been placed on the sides of the pillars and side walls.

Daylight falls into the hall mostly through the windows on the east side and the south front. In the evening, more than 3,000 light bulbs installed on six gilt chandeliers weighing 1.3 metric tons each and numerous wall lamps illuminate the hall. They have been fitted with electric bulbs since 1895. Before their installation, approximately 10,000 candles and 5,000 oil and petroleum lamps were required to light the festive halls.

More than 20 types of wood (including nutwood, mahogany, cherry, birch, oak, apple, pear, Karelian birch, and ebony) have been used to create a mosaic rich in patterns and symmetry on the parquet floor.

▷ View into St. George Hall from the north.

The State Parade Chambers

The suite known since its construction as the State or Catherine Apartment is located on the upper floor of the west wing of the Grand Kremlin Palace. It consists of smaller halls furnished with every imaginable extravagance, their doors precisely aligned. After passing through the Guard Hall in the southwest corner one enters large St. Catherine Hall, which together with the adjacent reception hall *(Cour d'honneur)* forms the main projection on the outer facade. The State Bedroom and the Dressing Room adjoin the Cour d'honneur.

▷ The main room in the State Parade Chambers, St. Catherine Hall, is named for the Order of St. Catherine founded by Peter I to honor women in 1714. The relatively small hall (21 meters long, 14 meters wide, 7 meters high) has two groined vaults supported by pilasters and piers at the windows. Konstantin Andreyevich Ton intended this hall to impress not by its size, but rather by its elegant proportions. Evidently, Ton attempted to create a festive yet peaceful atmosphere. The white ceiling and silver moiré wallpaper constitute a light, friendly color scheme in which a few bright spots of color (especially red) provide contrasts. Of course, there is also gold and the shimmer of other precious materials. The color red is repeated in the heraldic devices of the order and in the frames for the moiré panels. The drapery and the black marble pedestals of the huge crystal chandeliers set further accents. The pier and corner pilasters are covered with green malachite. The masterfully carved doors and cool shapes of the furniture bear traces of Classicism. On the whole, the furnishing of St. Catherine Hall is marked by a mixture of styles and a luxurious eclecticism which does not fail to fascinate the beholder with its shimmering splendor. The hall formerly served as a throne room; today the standing commissions of the Soviets of the Union and the Nationalities meet here. In addition, foreign delegations and heads of state and government are received in this room.

◁ The large State Hall is done in the Neo-Baroque style. Its ceilings were painted by Artari. The walls and gilt furniture are covered with green brocade interwoven with gold threads. The four tables with inlay work in the style of the Parisian carpenter Boule are especially valuable. Massive porcelain candelabra with flowerpots stand on gilt pedestals. They are of Japanese craftsmanship, whereas two other chandeliers are in the chinoiserie fashion. Two rosewood doors with mirrors and inlaid work open onto the room. A French clock stands on the mantel of the Carrara marble fireplace. The porcelain objects were produced by the Imperial Manufacture of St. Petersburg, most of the furniture by the St. Petersburg companies Peter Gambs and Andrei and Konstantin Tour, and the fabrics by the Muscovite purveyor to the court, G.G. Zaposhnikov.

△ Chair in the State Bedroom.

▷ ▷ View of the State Bedroom. The four-poster bed with canopy no longer exists. Otherwise, the State Bedroom has remained largely unchanged since it was built. A unique feature of this room are the monoliths; they are said to be the largest in all of Russia. On the open fireplace, which is covered with smoky greenish-blue Russian jade and has artificial marble columns, stands another product of the French art of clockmaking. Crystal chandeliers on pedestals of dark-red French marble and gold-plated doors in the Boule style are among the other luxury items in this hall. The purplish-red fabric on the furniture and walls replaces the original gold brocade.

The pompous furnishings of the State Parade Chambers also include excellent examples of the Western European art of clockmaking.

◁ The State Guest Bedroom. Open fireplace with French clock. In the foreground hangs a magnificent chandelier with crystal pendants.

△ Clock in Catherine Hall.

△ ▷ Open fireplace with clock flanked by candlesticks in the State Bedroom.

▷ Clock with a motif depicting the chariot of the sun on the open fireplace.

◁ A Russian-crafted standing mirror with an oak frame in the Dining Hall.

△ A cool Classicism is combined with the conciliatory Biedermeier style in the Dining Hall. The segmental elements and the foliate ornamentation on the reinforcing arches, friezes, and vaults are made of white stucco, and the panels on the pilasters, piers, and wall surfaces are of yellowish imitation marble with thin black veins. Among the noteworthy furnishings, which include marble vases with mythological motifs and Classic statues in the niches along the walls, special mention should be made of two huge porcelain vases (one of which can be seen on the right side of the photograph). Events from the history of Russia are depicted on the bellies of the heavily gilt vases. They were signed by leading potters and painters of the tsarist realm and dated 1827. The severity of the chairs covered with deep red morocco leather reflects the style of the 1880s.

The Private Apartments

(Private Chambers of the Tsar's Family)

On the ground floor of the south wing – under the present assembly room of the Supreme Soviet – is the so-called Private Apartments. It consists of an imposing seven-room suite in which the doors are all accurately lined up in one row: the Dining Room, the Tsaritsa's Reception Room, the Tsaritsa's Study, the Boudoir, the Bedchamber, the Tsar's Study, and the Tsar's Reception Room. Because the suite lies in the lower part of the Grand Palace, the statics of the building determined to a certain extent the floor plans of the rooms. A mighty row of piers divides the rooms, which are usually laid out along two axes. This row divides the rooms into two groups: a more formal area, located in the passage-like front section with the windows facing the Moskva, and a more private, intimate area behind and between the freestanding pillars.

The rooms in the Private Apartments are masterpieces of interior decoration. Although the medley of styles does not follow any strict pattern, the unmistakable, succinct form and atmosphere in each room testifies to the outstanding eclecticism of the interior decorators of that period and their unerring sense of style, rich imaginations, and good taste. They followed old traditions to some extent, yet also aspired to blend old forms with new fashions. Awesome is the extravagant use of materials; grandiose the combination of porcelain, crystal, and bronze decorations, the rare fabrics, and the stylized furniture with fantastic carvings and exquisite inlays.

▷ View of the row of rooms in the Private Apartments. In the foreground, the Tsaritsa's Guest or Reception Room.

◁ The Tsaritsa's Reception Room. In contrast to the Classic Dining Hall, the salon is done entirely in the Neo-Rococo manner. Peculiar to the interior is the light coloring and the graceful interplay of white, gold, and a little blue. The curved furniture contours, the frivolous gold ornamentation, the decorated silk wallpapers, and the extremely intricate stencil paintings on the geometrically accented pendentive dome all combine to produce a festive, elegant atmosphere. The photograph, taken in the direction of the windos, provides an impression of the layout of the rooms: the central pier stands between the chamber's passage section with its window front and the "private" area at the back (in the foreground of the photograph). A gilt wooden grille (at the right of the picture) sections off the private area, which was also called the "comfortable corner." The chandelier in the foreground with the hand-shaped porcelain flowers follows the tradition of great Russian ceramists, above all of the famous master P.U. Ivanov, who was employed in the imperial manufacture from 1808 to 1829. Some of the furniture is made of nutwood and rosewood encrusted with tortoiseshell and decorated with mother-of-pearl and inlays.

△ The porcelain vases, hanging lamps, and clocks in the salon are rarities. The intensive turquoise background color, the merry and erotic pastoral scenes, and the weightless world of the putti and flowers imitate the famous Sèvres porcelain from the mid-18th century.

The Tsaritsa's Study imitates French interiors of the late 17th and early 18th centuries. Because it has two central piers, the "comfortable corner" is a stately succession of room sections that are separated by islands of furniture – typical for the mid-19th century. The same shade of purple-red dominates the carpets and wallpaper. A contrast is provided by the classic order of pilasters made of white stucco with gilt ornamentation: flutes, scrolls, and palmettes on the capitals, friezes, reinforcing arches, and cross groins. The socle is covered with black marble. Huge crystal mirrors stand between the pilasters. Carrara marble decorates the fireplace. The huge hanging chandeliers were characteristically named "waterfalls." The furniture and the doors are partly made of nutwood and rosewood with bronze decorations.

▷ Grandfather clock in the Tsaritsa's Study.

217

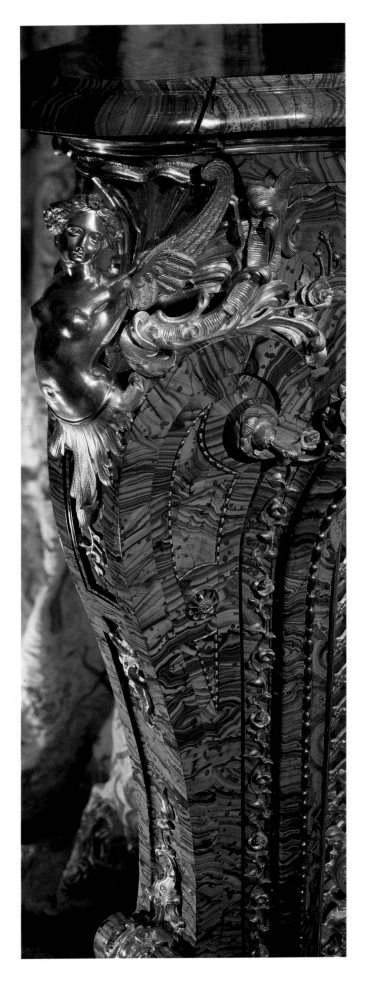

△ Clock on the mantelpiece of the Boudoir. French (Mathieu). This magnificent piece of complicated machinery stands on a pedestal and is contained in an amphora-like encasing of gilt bronze. Two revolving enameled rings, with the minutes indicated by Arabic numerals and the hours by Roman numerals, have been fitted around the edge of the housing. The tail of a lizard – a symbol of time – crawling underneath the rings serves as the hand. The round face in the pedestal shows the months, days of the week, and phases of the moon inside a ring of astrological signs.

◁ The open fireplace, artistically installed in one of the window piers, seems to be made of a monolith, but is in fact expertly put together of extremely thin layers of malachite. The addition of gilt bronze – here the cast figure of a siren between the volute and the mantelpiece – has a long tradition in Russia.

▷ The Tsaritsa's Boudoir was intended to serve as a room in which it was possible to withdraw and relax. The relatively intimate room is covered by two barrel vaults, one of which is above the corridor half of the room. Shades of gray and pink dominate the textiles for the furniture and wallpaper. The gilt decoration has been used only for small bands on the vertical walls, but was applied generously to the ceilings.

◁ The Tsar's Bedchamber. Dark blue dominates this room, in which the gilding has been concentrated in small bands and in the ornamentation of the ceiling, as in the Boudoir. A French clock stands on the mantel of Carrara marble; its mechanism is encased in a starred globe as black as the night.

△ Chair in the Adjutant's Waiting Room. The satin upholstery is an earthy bronze color with brownish plant motifs. The particularly artistic cuts of velvet produce variable light and shadow effects. All fabrics of this type used in the Kremlin were produced in the Moscow factory of the Zaposhnikov Brothers.

▷ The Tsar's Study radiates severity and officialdom. Two large desks, several chairs of a pronounced upright form, and a narrow sofa furnish the room. Light-colored wood from oak trees and Karelian birches is combined with green cloth and black morocco leather. The wall panels conceal bookshelves that formerly held the collection of laws in the tsarist realm. This was the sole library in the entire Kremlin. Insulating hollow spaces in the walls made this room an island of peace and concentration amidst the hustle and bustle of the tsarist court.

The Chamber of the Supreme Soviet of the USSR

This imposing hall is located in the main section of the building above the Private Apartments. Its windows face south towards the Moskva River. The hall was created in 1934, when the magnificent St. Andrew and St. Alexander Halls were combined under the supervision of Illarion Alexandrovich Ivanov-Shitz.

The chamber of the Supreme Soviet is both majestic and simple. Its white walls, segmented by pilasters, the high, round-arched windows, and the flat dome with its coffered ceiling lend the room an impression of spaciousness.

Equipment for simultaneous translation has been installed in the nutwood chairs covered with morocco leather on the parquet. Boxes for the press, the diplomatic corps, and other guests are available in the balconies. Toward the end of the 1950s the formerly open platform was turned into a winter garden, thus renewing the tradition of hanging gardens that started in Moscow in the 17th century.

Several monuments in the Grand Kremlin Palace serve as reminders of Vladimir Lenin's significant works, including a marble statue in the parliamentary chamber created by Sergei Merkurov in 1939. The State Parade Chambers of the Grand Kremlin Palace is still chiefly used for state affairs today. It provides the appropriate framework for the official receptions of foreign guests as well as the meetings of commissions and committees of the Soviet parliament. Until 1970, foreign ambassadors presented their credentials in the former Dining Hall (on the ground floor) and St. Catherine Hall (on the second floor). The Committee for the International Lenin Peace Prize still meets in the state parade rooms.

△ View from the entrance of the Chamber of the Supreme Soviet of the USSR, which is located on the upper floor of the south wing and thus above the Private Apartments. Its dimensions are impressive: 78 meters long and 20 meters wide. The statue of Lenin created in 1939 stands in the middle niche on the western wall.

Restorations in the Grand Kremlin Palace

A comprehensive and ambitious restoration program was carried out in the Grand Kremlin Palace from 1966 to 1969. In three short years, all of the state rooms were refurbished. But this was not all: the supporting structures were stabilized, modern pipes and cables were laid, and the decor was reproduced true to the original, which had been partly destroyed and partly changed by later redesigning. In St. George Hall, the massive, masterfully inlaid door had to be repaired and the stuccowork on the clerestory protected.

The regilding of the decorations in the state rooms of the palace posed special problems. Experts form Leningrad revived the forgotten technique of gilding an a red ocher base, which produced an inimitable decorative effect. The luxurious decor, especially the gilding of the state rooms of the State Parade Chambers, could thus be restored not only with the care it deserved but also according to the highest technical standards.

The renovation of the parquet floor in St. George Hall, which was conducted according to original 19th-century drawings by Feodor Grigoryevich Zolntsev, also presented serious problems. Rare precious woods such as oriental plane, beech, ash, Indian rosewood, and African padauk required treatment, and the retouched area measured 1,200 square meters.

In the conference hall of the new palace building – the present chamber of the Soviet parliament – the chairs of the presidium had to be mounted on new steel girders, the boxes for the diplomats enlarged, and new floors laid on the parquet and balcony levels. New air conditioning and a new lighting system were also installed.

▷ Detail of a restoration. Around 1970, parts of the carved stone ornamentation on one portal in Terem Palace were uncovered, revealing the original coloration from the 17th century. The naked white stone is visible at the left and the portal's condition before cleaning at the right. The middle section shows the reproduction of the original polychrome coloring with red and green backgrounds. The dirt at the right was caused chiefly by the frequent use of the chamber and its illumination with candles.

In the Chamber of Facets, a team of experts from Kiev remade and gilt a part of the old portal, repaired the layers of plaster and paint, and relaid the parquet floor. The central pier of the Chamber of Facets was reinforced by a metal structure. These restorations also turned up valuable finds for art historians; for example, N. Pomerantsev discovered a fragment of stucco from the 15th century on the central pier. Specialists from Kiev restored the Holy Vestibule, the Parade Stairway, the Antechamber, and St. Vladimir Hall, paying special attention to the artistic parquet floor. During the work carried out in 1968, the facades of the three upper stories of Terem Palace were restored to their original beauty and the polychrome decorations of the windows were reproduced. However, the interior decorations in Terem Palace could be restored only to their 19th-century state, with the inclusion of a few older fragments.

The restorations in the Grand Kremlin Palace were not only comprehensive, but also extremely complicated in technique. A wide range of techniques and specialist crafts were applied, such as assembling the parquet floors, doing inlay work on the doors, making furniture in styles from past centuries, repairing products of the applied arts, and eliminating the extensive damage that had befallen details of the palace decor over the centuries. Painters, architects, sculptors, artistic carpenters, and specialists for gilding and for producing ceramics and rare textiles came from Moscow, Leningrad, Kiev, Odessa, Yaroslavl, and other cities of the great Soviet Union and passed this difficult and unique test of their abilities with flying colors.

The architectural ensemble of the Grand Kremlin Palace represents a link between past and present in the Kremlin, because even today it plays a highly significant role in the history of the Soviet Union. The Supreme Soviet of the USSR (the parliament) holds its sessions in the Grand Kremlin Palace. Before the Palace of Congress was built in the Kremlin, several conventions of the CPSU (Communist Party of the Soviet Union) took place here. Foreign heads of state and government are received here, and negotiations and talks with delegations from Communist and other political parties from many countries are conducted.

△ Example of a restoration. The cleaning of the painted fabric icons from the Church of the Resurrection in the Grand Kremlin Palace requires specialized knowledge and meticulous work. A team from the restoration workshops of the Kremlin Museums is shown at work here.

Pages 230/31: View from the dome-shaped roof with flagpole on the south wing of the Grand Kremlin Palace towards Cathedral Square (at the right, with the Belfry) and the Terem wing (at the left; behind it, the new Palace of Congress).

229

The Amusement Palace

The Amusement Palace, located on the west side of the Kremlin between Troitskaia and Commandant Towers, dates from the 17th century. In 1652, the boyar I. Miloslavski had a pompous palace of several stories erected. After his death, the palace fell to the state and was redesigned for theatrical productions and amusements by order of Alexei Mikhailovich. Thenceforth it was known as the Amusement Palace, although the tower-shaped upper part of the building originally served as a private chapel. A small watch and alarm tower on four columns above the refectory still catches the eye. There has been no lack of alterations: in the 1870s, a balcony on vase-shaped columns was added on the side facing the Kremlin wall; another addition is the magnificent white stone portal with carved ornamentation in the 17th-century Russian style on the side facing the street.

The shift from the severe, reserved architecture of the 15th to the 16th century to the magnificent and varied forms of the 17th century is especially obvious in the Moscow Kremlin, a fact that greatly increases its value as a monument.

▷ The name "Amusement Palace" follows Western European designations. The building was used chiefly for plays and other amusements. The façade was restored under the direction of K.A. Ton from 1874 to 1875. The window settings, with their powerful ornamentation, columns, and open gables, still remain from the older central building, yet they, too, were radically altered in the 19th century to suit the new style of the Terem façade.

233

The Patriarchal Palace and the Church of the Twelve Apostles

The Patriarchal Palace (the best-preserved 17th-century secular building in the Kremlin) and the Church of the Twelve Apostles are located on the northwest side of Cathedral Square. The palace was erected from 1652 to 1655 for Patriarch Nikon, on an older foundation dating from the 15th or 16th century, after the Church of the Miracle-Worker of Zolovtsy had been torn down and the area of Boris Godunov's former courtyard cleared. The simple, modest exterior formed a marked contrast to the luxurious, colorful architecture of the chambers of the largest landowner in Russia at the time. Private chambers lay close to state rooms and monastery cells in the palace. Numerous narrow stairways and corridors connected the rooms in the imaginative manner so characteristic of Russian residential architecture. The Chamber of the Cross covered an impressive 280 square meters. Paul of Aleppo, a high church official from Syria who was invited to the dedication of the new Patriarchal Palace, reported enthusiastically that the unusual spaciousness of the Chamber of the Cross surprised the visitor. He admired the large vault with no central support; along the walls, steps had been built so that the room seemed to be a basin without water, especially as it was covered with wonderfully colored tiles. Paul thought it sensible that the chamber's large windows, with the enchanting isinglass panes, should be turned toward the church. The councils of the Orthodox Church met in this gala chamber, where the highest church dignitaries were received and the great festivals celebrated.

A private chapel adjoins the Patriarchal Palace to the east. Although it was built at the same time as the palace, it was not known as the Church of the Twelve Apostles until 1681. Immediately after the church's construction, its walls were painted, an expensive iconostasis was created and glazed, and blue-green tiles were laid on the floor.

The large fire in 1682 caused extensive damage to the palace and the church. Toward the end of the 17th century, the Kremlin experienced a new surge of building activity. Presumably, Patriarch Andrian had the open gallery built on massive piers on the north side during this time. The upper story of the palace was added in 1691. Other changes in and around the Patriarchal Palace were made in the following centuries, especially as the edifice fell under the jurisdiction of the synod. In 1720, a sacristy and a new iconostasis were added to the church; at the end of the 18th century, architect Matvei Feodorovich Kazakov altered a few rooms in the palace – above all, the Chamber of the Cross. After 1763, *miro* (a fragrant oil) was made every three years in the Chamber of the Cross for all Russian churches, which thereafter lent the chamber the name "miro brewery."

△ View of the south front of the Patriarchal Palace and the Church of the Twelve Apostles. The compact building displays the new severeness and monumentality that replaced the colorful church façades of the 17th century in Russia. The five-domed form of the church roof goes back to the Uspenskii Cathedral in Vladimir, as do the decorative blind arches on the cupola drums.

235

The Museum of 17th-Century Applied Arts is now located on the first floor of the former Patriarchal Palace. It houses over 1,000 exhibits from the storerooms of the Armory. Robes made of valuable fabrics, exquisite jewelry, dishes for festive occasions and daily life, and a large number of household utensils convey some idea of the way of life of Russian tsars, boyars, and high church officials. The collection of printed and handwritten documents is also of great worth and illustrates the history of printing in Russia. It includes the primer titled *Medicine for the Soul* written by Larion Isomin for Tsarevich Alexei, the son of Peter I, as well as a printed psalter from 1591.

Connoisseurs and laymen alike will take an interest in the collections of Russian and foreign clocks (from the late 16th to the early 17th century) and the astoundingly well-crafted toys of silver, amber, ivory, and tortoiseshell. Special mention is due the extraordinary collection of clothes and utensils for the "Royal Games" (falconry and goshawk-hunting, hunting bears with spears, and driving foxes and deer). The collection of old furniture, chests and trunks, and candles and chandeliers provides an accurate idea of what the interiors of the palace chambers must have looked like.

The Patriarchal Palace and the Church of the Twelve Apostles were the first buildings to be examined and restored in the Kremlin. In 1922, a walled porch with a richly decorated column was discovered on the north side of the church. Subsequently, the arched carriage-ways through the building were unwalled. The gilt iconostasis (from the first third of the 18th century) was moved from the former Monastery of the Ascension to the Church of the Twelve Apostles in 1929).

During restoration work on Cathedral Square in the summer of 1955, the arched passages leading through the palace to the former Patriarchal Courtyard were completely opened up. In the 1950s and '60s it became possible to faithfully restore numerous architectural details, murals, elements of the carvings on the iconostasis, and the inlaid table. In the 1970s and '80s the foundation was stabilized, the palace and church roofs repaired, and the wooden supports over the Chamber of the Cross replaced by metal ones. At the same time, the collections in the museums were reorganized.

▷ Trio of windows with thick ogee-shaped arches on the north front of the Patriarchal Palace. The four-story building was designed in the 17th century style of Moscow architecture, whereas the art of Suzdal-Vladimir survives in the decoration.

The Senate Building

Every one of the monuments in the Moscow Kremlin occupies a significant position in the history of Russian architecture. In the 18th century, many renowned architects worked in the Kremlin. From 1749 to 1753, the famous Bartolomeo Rastrelli erected a new winter palace of stone for Empress Yelizaveta Petrovna in place of several razed buildings from the 15th and 17th centuries on the southern slope of Borovitskii Hill. During the reign of Catherine II, plans were made to build a huge new palace on the same site. V. Bazhenov, a well-known Russian architect, worked with the young architect Matvei Feodorovich Kazakov on this project starting in 1767. Extensive preparations had already been carried out, some old buildings torn down, and the construction site cleared. In 1773 the foundation was laid. But political and financial difficulties forced the Russian government to stop construction in 1775. The daring project of one of the most talented Russian architects in the 18th century remained unfulfilled.

In 1776, construction of the Senate Building was begun according to plans by Kazakov on a small and rather inconvenient building site opposite the Arsenal. It was completed in 1787, and its wonderful dome has ever since been one of Moscow's landmarks. The building was originally intended for meetings of the Muscovite nobility. When two departments of the Senate were transferred from Petrograd to Moscow in the 1920s, the building was turned over to the Moscow Senate. The court of justice has been located in this building since 1856. In order to prevent any misunderstandings, a statue with a crown and the inscription "Law" were placed on the dome as emblems of the jurisdiction of the tsarist state. When the Soviet government moved into the Kremlin on March 11, 1918, this building became the seat of government. The Commandant of the Kremlin at that time, P. Malkov, reports that Lenin himself personally gave the order to hoist the red flag above the cupola of the building, which had become the property of the Soviet of People's Commissars. The staff of the first Soviet government was so small that it did not fill even half the rooms of this huge edifice. A school for the children of Kremlin personnel existed in the right wing of the building from 1921 to 1924. Later, the building was renamed and called the Building of the Government of the USSR. For many years it was the seat of the head of state, the chairman of the Presidium of the Supreme Soviet of the USSR, the vice-chairman, and the secretary of the Presidium, as well as the chairmen of the Councils of the Union and the Nationalities. Today, the Cabinet of the USSR is housed here.

△ The Senate Building is among the best works of Matvei Kazakov, an outstanding representative of Classicism in Russian architecture. He was actively assisted by I. Zelechov, I. Yegotov, and K. Polivanov, respected Russian architects. The early Classic style of this edifice blends harmoniously with the older architectural ensemble of the Kremlin and the city. Kazakov skillfully placed sections of the building within the triangle formed by the outer wings, thus forming a pentagonal inner courtyard. Despite its considerable length, the three story edifice has a graceful appearance, not least due to its tall windows and the Doric order. The walls are placed at such angles to one another that the façades appear to merge smoothly. The main entrance to the inner courtyard was designed as a majestic Ionic portal with ornamental gables, four columns, and a rather low dome. It is located directly opposite the raised portal of the Arsenal. A spacious rectangular square was formed between both buildings; the charming St. Nicholas Tower marks its northern side. Originally, it was named Senate Square; later, it became Arsenal Square. Today it is called I. Kalyayev Square.

One of the attractions in the Senate Building is certainly St. Catherine Hall (now called Sverdlov Hall), a mighty domed chamber built for the assemblies of the boyar parliament. Rows of columns topped by Classic friezes line the facade on the ground and second floors. A half-circle of wide steps leads to the main entrance, which is decorated with a Classic portico. Twenty-four Corinthian columns line the chamber itself. They support an open gallery on which a mighty drum vault with a coffered ceiling and stucco rosettes rests. The vault measures 24.7 meters in diameter and is 27 meters high at its crown. A vault this large had never been seen in late 18th-century Russia before, so that contemporaries respectfully named it the Russian Pantheon. The hall was renamed Sverdlov Hall after the Soviet Union's first head of state, Yakov Sverdlov, who died in March 1919.

During the first few years following the Revolution, Sverdlov Hall served as a club for the Kremlin personnel and officer-trainees and as a room where various party conventions and conferences took place. Shortly after his death in 1925, a marble bust of Lenin was placed behind the platform as a reminder of these events. Today, Sverdlov Hall is the scene of plenary sessions of the Central Committee of the CPSU and of award ceremonies for Lenin and state prizes, as well as for the highest national honors.

Time has also left its mark on this hall. Its overall appearance, its interior decorations, and the colors of its walls were frequently altered to suit the tastes of the different periods. Restorations in the 1960s reproduced the hall's original appearance. The walls were painted light blue, the rosettes gilded, the bas-reliefs cleaned, and blue drapes hung in the windows.

The Oval Hall is located on the same floor, a relatively small and modest light-green chamber with Renaissance decorations and snow-white imitations of antique medallions that emphasize the general intimacy of its atmosphere. The hall was restored with a great deal of both intuition and expert knowledge in 1965–1966. Today it is used for plenary sessions of the Central Committee of the CPSU and meetings of various government panels.

▷ View into the circular cupola with absolutely symmetrical decorations.

▽ View of Sverdlov Hall in the Senate Building. The areas between the windows of the cupola drum are covered with medallions of Russian princes and tsars. They are plaster copies of the marble bas-reliefs created by Feodor Ivanovich Shubin, the renowned Russian sculptor, in 1774–1775 and now housed in the Armory. Eighteen stucco high reliefs form part of the frieze above the round-arched windows. They were made by Gavril Tikhanovich Zamarayev in honor of Empress Catherine II and portray scenes from her reign. The other decorations were created by Yust and Arnoldi, two respected Russian sculptors.

The rooms where Vladimir I. Lenin lived for over five years, and from which he directed the affairs of state, represent an incomparable attraction for many citizens of the Soviet Union. They now form the museum "Office and Private Rooms of V. Lenin in the Kremlin." After the Soviet government moved to Moscow, the second floor of the Senate Building was put at the disposal of the Soviet of People's Commissars (the Cabinet). The office of Lenin, the Chairman, was located in one of the six rooms leading one into another adjacent to his private apartment.

Lenin worked in this office from March 19, 1918, to December 12, 1922. The Kremlin period of his life is characterized by the extremely important decisions he had to make as well as by the hard work he did to stabilize and build up the young Soviet republic. Lenin's repeated efforts to support the preservation and restoration of the art and historical monuments in the Kremlin during these difficult years are remarkable, especially because these monuments had been created under a rule despised by the revolutionaries. Lenin met visitors from throughout the world in his office every day. Workers and peasants came to Moscow from far away to ask him for advice and assistance. The leader of the Revolution also received outstanding personages: politicians, diplomats, journalists, authors, businessmen, and party cadre were constantly going in and out of his office.

▷ Excellent photograph of Lenin taken around 1920 by an unknown photographer. Glass plate print.

◁ Lenin's former office is a light, spacious room with a high vaulted roof. His desk, a long table for visitors covered with a dark red cloth and four leather lounge chairs, stood next to a large tile stove in the corner. Lenin himself preferred a simple wooden chair with a canework back and seat. Two revolving bookshelves are located on both sides of the desk and hold various reference works, shorthand reports from party congresses, papers from the conferences and congresses of the Comintern, foreign-language dictionaries, V. Dal's defining dictionary of the Russian language, and newspapers and magazines. There are a tremendous number of books and maps: Lenin's private library contained over 10,000 books and brochures that reflect the variety of his interests. Lenin usually read foreign books and newspapers in their original languages.

△ One door leads from Lenin's office to the telephone exchange upstairs and another leads to the conference room (photo above), where meetings of the Soviet of People's Commissars and the Soviet of Work and Defense were held and plenary sessions of the Central Committee and the Politburo took place. Visitors were also received in this room at that time. In the 1930s, the hall was refinished and enlarged by incorporating an adjacent room. Sessions of the Cabinet of the USSR, party organs, and various national committees met here until 1958. A white marble statue of Lenin (sculpted by N. Andreyev) was set up here in 1974.

At the end of March 1918, Lenin's family moved into a small, modestly furnished four-room apartment on the second floor of the Senate Building. M. Averbach, a member of the Academy of Sciences and a frequent guest of the Ulyanov-Lenin family, reported that Lenin was satisfied with this small apartment. It had, so Averbach said, just the number of rooms required by Lenin and his relatives, who also had responsible positions in the society. Averbach continued that, as soon as one opened the door to Lenin's apartment, one could tell by the furnishings that the head of the household was a man of great intelligence and moderation. Everything was simple, clean, and in its place. There was no trace of unnecessary splendor or objects of luxury that one did not really know what to do with, whereas one could find everything that a family living from work and intellectual interests required.

Lenin's sister, Maria Ulyanova, lived in the largest room, and his wife, Nadesha Krupskaia, had the adjoining one. The next room belonged to Vladimir Lenin. The fourth room – actually the living room – had to be turned into a sickroom after Lenin was wounded in the attempt on his life an August 30, 1918. Nadesha Krupskaia and Maria Ulyanova remained in the apartment to the ends of their lives and took pains to keep up the furnishings and atmosphere that had existed during Lenin's lifetime.

After the deaths of Lenin's relatives, work on a Lenin Memorial was begun in the Kremlin at the end of 1939. By April 1955, the authentic appearance of the office had been reproduced. Since then, everything connected to Lenin's work and life in the Kremlin has been carefully retained, cared for, and restored.

△ The "Doctor's Room," in which Lenin's brother, Dmitrii Ilyich, lived. It did not belong to the actual Lenin family apartment. In 1980, it was restored and became part of the museum. One of Lenin's favorite pieces of music, the rondo allegro from the "Sonate pathétique" by Ludwig van Beethoven, lies open on the grand piano.

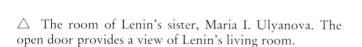

△ The room of Lenin's sister, Maria I. Ulyanova. The open door provides a view of Lenin's living room.

◁ Lenin's bed-sitting room. A photograph of Lenin and Nadesha Krupskaia hangs over the bed.

▷ Detail of Nadesha Krupskaia's room. On the table is a picture of Lenin of which she was especially fond, as well as an album she had made of some of her favorite photographs.

The Building of the Presidium of the Supreme Soviet of the USSR

(Government Building)

After construction of the Kremlin Palace of Congress was completed (in 1961), the old Kremlin theater building in front of Spasskii Gate was assigned to the Presidium of the Supreme Soviet of the USSR, the directing body of the Soviet parliament.

This edifice has undergone several alterations during the years of Soviet rule. Many old, rather decrepit secular and ecclesiastical buildings in this part of the Kremlin proved to be unsuitable for the seat of the highest government organ. In 1929, small Nicholas Palace (built by Kazakov in the 18th century and changed considerably in the 19th century) was therefore torn down, followed by Chudov (Miracle-Worker) and Voznessenye (Ascension) Monasteries in 1932 – 1934. A new building for a military academy that trained officers for the Kremlin garrison was erected on the site. The project originated with Ivan Ivanovich Rerberg. The south front, which faced the Moskva, was built on the same spot as the south wall of Kazakov's palace. The architect planned the proportions and colors to harmonize with the nearby former Senate Building. According to the fashion at the turn of the century, the building was designed in an extremely simple, neo-classic style. Three parallel blocks were placed next to the facade of the building's main body along the east part of the Kremlin wall. The neo-classic front, with a portico including eight Ionic columns, is a remarkable piece of architecture.

In 1958, A. Hokhlyakov redesigned the offices and main hall as a comfortable, modern, yet somewhat small theater with 1,200 seats. Twenty years later, the whole building was remade into the seat of the Soviet Parliament by a team of architects led by Mikhail Vassilye-vich Possokhin. Only the original layout of the rooms remained untouched. Care was taken to furnish their interiors in accordance with the requirements of their present functions and uses. Two side stairways lead from an airy vestibule to the main lobby and from there to the hall used by both chambers of parliament: the Soviets of the Union and the Nationalities. Large, elongated windows, white columns, festive crystal chandeliers, and a light-colored parquet floor create a distinctive atmosphere.

▷ Entrance projection with portico on the main front (facing southeast) of the Government Building.

Pages 252/53: The Vestibule.

The chamber of the Soviets of the Union and of the Nationalities forms the structural core of the building. A change in the room's axis and complicated engineering operations were required in redoing this hall. The room's interior had to fulfill the demands placed on it as the seat of the country's highest legislative body in a worthy and functionally appropriate manner. The 900 seats for the delegates are arranged before the presidium platform like an amphitheater. Behind them are boxes for guests and the foreign press; in the balcony above the amphitheater are the diplomats' boxes. The white ribbed marble walls appear light and cheerful thanks to gold-colored metal strips. Together with the dark burgundy of the furniture and the light gray of the thick pile carpet, the walls create a festive and distinctive color scheme. A sense of fantasy is displayed by the structure of the drop ceiling and the elegant, wheel-shaped crystal lamp (2 meters in diameter, 1.5 metric tons in weight, with 1,500 light bulbs). The third rather large room is the conference room for the Presidium, a spacious rectangular hall. It opens into the office of the Chairman of the Presidium of the Supreme Soviet – the Soviet head of government. In a side room, the numerous gifts from foreign state and parliamentary delegations are displayed.

On the second floor of the building a stately, imposing suite of rooms continues the traditions of the Moscow Kremlin in an up-to-date way and successfully combines them with the modern architectural and technical installations. The first room is an entrance hall that leads into a reception room for foreign ambassadors and delegations. The last is the conference room for the head of state, where foreign delegations are officially received.

△ Chamber of the Soviets of the Union and of the Nationalities in the Government Building.

▷ Insignia of the Soviets of the Union and of the Nationalities.

The Palace of Congress

In the 1960s, a monumental palace was built next to Troiskaia Tower that became the largest public building in the Soviet Union. Construction work proceeded rapidly. The new palace arose in less than two years on the site of old barracks and the old Armory Building, so that the 22nd Congress of the CPSU was able to convene there on October 17, 1961. A team of architects and engineers was awarded the Lenin Prize for the planning and execution of the construction work.

The key architectural problem consisted of integrating the modern Palace of Congress into the Kremlin ensemble. Unenclosed inner areas were preferred in order to fulfill this requirement. This openness also makes it possible to connect the rooms of all the functionally different areas. Elevators, escalators, and stairways join the floors and various sections (the congress wing, the lobby and stairway, and the office wing) to form a large functional and architectural unit. One can survey the entire complex from the escalators and, at the same time, take a look at the Kremlin's architectural monuments through the huge panes of glass from an unusual perspective.

The main lobby links all of the interior rooms and functional areas. The broad frieze of reddish-gold smalt contains a mosaic by Alexander Alexandrovich Deineka. Another mosaic by Nikolai Ivanovich Bratsun and Yurii Grigoryevich Orezhov can be seen on the façade of the diplomatic corps wing. Not many large works of art are contained in the Palace of Congress, but those few harmonize tactfully and tastefully with the simple, majestic architectural forms. The semiprecious stones used in the decorations provide a variegated and impressive range of colors. All encasing materials – stone, wood, and fabric – as well as the colors, illumination, and even the many plants and trees conform to the architectural unity.

Concrete, steel, glass, and other modern building materials were used to build a palace of sparse, contemporary architectural expression, resulting in a severe silhouette and a terse yet eloquent interior. Its rib-like eaves rest on triangular piers of white marble, between which broad glass walls accentuate the mass of the entire edifice while still appearing light and airy. The clear-cut rhythm of the supports shows off the vertical segmentation of the building, whereas the balanced horizontal lines of the stories suit the contours of the Classic style of the Arsenal opposite. Located at the west edge of the Kremlin grounds, the Palace of Congress blends harmoniously into its unique surroundings. Because it is not taller than the surrounding buildings, it does not destroy the picturesque Kremlin silhouette. However, the building was sunk 15–16 meters into the ground in order to fulfill the demands placed on it. The cloakrooms and most of the offices are underground. A passage designed as a winter garden connects the Palace of Congress with the Grand Kremlin Palace. On the east, the building of the diplomatic corps adjoins the Palace of Congress and in its turn leads to the Patriarchal Palace. The main entrance is decorated with the USSR national coat of arms made of engraved gilt copper. The marble surfaces of the outside wall between the edges of the windows are adorned with mosaics of gold-colored smalt.

Pages 258/59: The main hall of the Palace of Congress.

257

The heart of the palace complex is the congress wing and its main hall, which has been flexibly designed to suit the many demands placed on it. The scattered yet expressive artistic decorations, modern encasing material, comfortable chairs, and appropriate lighting combine with the tasteful coloring in rich gold and red tones to lend this hall an unmistakable flair. The stage in the main hall, conceived and equipped for congresses as well as for entertainment, incorporates a very high level of technology. The front stage, for the Presidium, can be separated from the main stage by a fireproof partition. This partition is a panel made of thin, engraved sheets of metal (designed by the Latvian artists K. Ryssin and A. Melnikov). It displays the red flag and the image of Lenin in the rays of the rising sun, thus providing a stirring background that suits the basic furnishing of the hall.

The second largest hall in the Palace of Congress, the Banquet Hall above the main hall, can be used equally well for receptions and concerts. Its terraced floor imparts a rather unusual sense of space. As in all rooms in the palace except the main hall, a muted, soft combination of colors was chosen for the Banquet Hall (blue carpets, green stage curtains, silver-gray marble on the walls and for the columns). Thanks to glass walls, the room appears larger and provides a wonderful view of the Kremlin and the Soviet capital city.

Although it was conceived as an assembly hall for party conventions, the Palace of Congress is also well suited for international congresses, large festive affairs, rallies, and theater presentations and shows, as well as for receptions and banquets, large dances, and New Year's parties.

▷ Old meets new in the Moscow Kremlin. The golden domes of the churches and cathedrals are reflected in the glass walls of the Palace of Congress.

The Arsenal

The Arsenal extends along the west wall of the Kremlin between the Troitskaia and Nikolskaia Towers. Dmitrii Ivanov and Christopher Conrad began construction of the building in 1701 on order of Peter I. The work lasted decades: it was soon stopped because of the Great Northern War and was not resumed until 1722. Construction was finally completed in 1736. Yet the year after, a terrible fire at Pentecost greatly impaired the building. Not until 1787 did Girardi repair and rebuild it. After the War of 1812, the building again lay in ruins until Feodor Kirillovich Zolokov started to rebuild it in its present form in 1817.

Originally, the Arsenal was intended for the manufacture of weapons and the storage of military equipment. In addition, the armor and orders captured from the enemy in battle were to be displayed there as a sort of chronicle of the victories of Russian weapons. This explains why numerous military insignia in the form of stucco and relief decorations adorn the walls. A later plan called for the Arsenal to be turned into a Museum of the Patriotic War of 1812. Although this desire was never realized, over 800 French cannons captured by Russian troops and partisans during the retreat of Napoleon's army from Russia are lined up outside along the southeast wall. The barrels of the cannons were cast of bronze in Paris, Lyon, and Wroclaw between 1790 and 1810. Next to these cannons, some made by renowned Russian masters like Andrei Chokhov ("Troilius," 1590), Martyan Ossipov ("Gamayun," 1690), Yakov Dubina ("Wolf," 1659), and others are displayed. The huge double windows and their ornamental encasings on the Arsenal façade contrast rhythmically with the imposing yellow walls. The splendid portal at the main entrance to the Arsenal strengthens this feeling of majesty.

Most of the contemporary restoration work was carried out in the Arsenal in the 1970s. In 1977 the restoration of the facade was finished, the structural elements were stabilized, the inner and outer walls were reinforced, several architectural details were reproduced, and the metal gate was repaired. On both sides of the Arsenal gate, near Troitskaia Tower, new memorial plaques of white marble were attached: on the right, in honor of the Arsenal soldiers who were shot by counterrevolutionary officer-trainees on October 28, 1917, and on the left, in honor of the soldiers of the Kremlin garrison who fell defending Moscow and the Kremlin in World War II. The Russian and French cannons lined up on pedestals along the Arsenal walls also had to be restored with specially developed techniques, which revealed hidden elements of the decoration, coats of arms, and inscriptions.

▷ The east front of the Arsenal as seen from the south, with Nikolskaia Tower in the background.

Pages 264/65: The "Unicorn" cannon. Decorative carriage from the 19th century.

△ The Tsar Cannon, a masterpiece of Russian casting. It was cast of bronze by Andrei Chokhov in 1586 and stands in front of the Church of the Twelve Apostles. Its weight of 40 metric tons, length of 5.34 meters, and 890-millimeter caliber made it the largest cannon in the world at that time. It supposedly could fire cartridges in accordance with military requirements, yet it never fired a single shot. Because it was supposed to defend the Kremlin, the Tsar Cannon stood on Red Square for many years. Not until 1835 were a carriage and three decorative cannonballs made for the cannon in St. Petersburg. At that time, the cannon was placed

as a museum exhibit near the old Armory building in front of the Arsenal. When the Palace of Congress was built in the Kremlin, the Tsar Cannon was moved to its present position. In the winter of 1980, the cannon and its carriage had to leave the Kremlin: during the course of time it, too, had become in need of repair. After many layers of paint had been removed and the metal treated according to a specially developed method, the old cannon was returned to its place in the Moscow Kremlin.

▷ Detail of the cannon "The New Persian."

▷ View of the old Armory. Engraving from the early 19th century.

History of the Armory

The origin of the collections in the famed Armory – even the individual exhibits – reflect the political history of the Grand Princedom of Moscow and the Russian nation. The unique exhibition dates back to the late Middle Ages, when the Muscovite grand princes increased their political influence and wealth considerably. Slowly, the development of a centralized state, the rapid economic rise and the Kremlin's strong international contacts led to the accumulation of inestimable riches. Whereas only a few valuables belonged to Grand Prince Ivan Kalita's estate (d. 1341) according to the records from 1358, a mere hundred years later reports told of numerous overflowing trunks and chests stored in the cathedrals and palaces of the Kremlin.

Many building projects were carried out under Ivan III (1462–1505): old wooden structures were replaced by fortifications, defense towers and terem palaces were made of white stone. Cultural contacts filled the privy treasury of the princes with valuable works by Russian and international artists and artisans, precious gold and silver objects, jewels, gold embroideries, and exquisite sable and marten furs. Only the most valuable, most beautiful, most unusual treasures were good enough for the Kremlin: coats of armor; tableware made of precious metals; clothing decorated with diamonds, rubies and emeralds, gems of an exquisite beauty; foreign jewelry encrusted with all shades of amber, mother-of-pearl and jasper and with colorful enamel work and bright ornaments; the choicest gold embroideries and the loveliest Russian icons.

Ivan III had a special storage-place built for the valuables in 1485: the Treasure House. For almost four centuries this brick building, located on Cathedral Square in the middle of the Kremlin, housed the most important riches of the Kremlin – yet by no means all of them. Not only majestic cathedrals and imposing palaces stood behind the Kremlin walls, but also numerous workshops, the "cabinets." All of the objects used to decorate the palaces and form the luxurious settings for receiving foreign emissaries and for religious ceremonies, military parades, and imperial hunts were manufactured in these workshops. Ceremonial etiquette became increasingly complicated, formal, and rigid, leading to a demand for more cabinets and in turn resulting in an ever more confusing system of workshops.

The following departments today can be distinguished among the huge, medieval workshop complex: the actual Armory (Oruzheinaia Palata), the oldest and largest workshop in Russia, which produced cut-and-thrust weapons, firearms, and all sorts of

▷ Old view of one of the collection halls. This is the Hall of Tableware as pictured in a late 19th-century print by B. Bachmann.

Pages 272/73: View of the front (facing southeast) of the Armory built by Konstantin Andreyevich Ton from 1844–1851.

270

271

armor; the Treasure House *(kazennyi dvor)*, where treasures and the regalia of the Muscovite rulers and the state were stored and repaired; the Office of Stables *(konushennyi prikaz)*, which was responsible for the court stables as well as the manufacture of riding equipment and bridles for daily use and ceremonial occasions, and whose customers included the tsar's bodyguard as well as the tsar himself; the Chamber of the Tsaritsa *(masterskaia* or *postelnaia palata)*, which attended to the sewing, decoration, and care of wardrobes, the production of gold and silver lace, and the embroidery of veils; the Hall of Gold and Silver, which provided the court and the patriarchs with the symbols of their positions and jewelry; and finally, the Office of Icons *(ikonnyi prikaz)*, which employed the best painters in Russia.

The largest and oldest department of the Kremlin workshops was the weapons factory, the Armory, which later gave the museum its name. As of the 16th century, a growing number of reports from astonished travelers and chroniclers stated that the treasury in the Moscow Kremlin was unbelievably rich and contained treasures of an incomparable beauty. Ivan IV (the Terrible) made a point of impressing his guests and foreign envoys with its magnificence and wealth. An English merchant reported the following after an audience with the tsar in 1553: "The tsar sat on his throne, a golden diadem on his head and clothed in an exceedingly splendid robe on which gold embroideries sparkled like fire. In his right hand he held a golden scepter encrusted with jewels. At the sides of the throne stood dignitaries in incredibly magnificent robes … This brilliance must necessarily blind anyone." A German envoy staying in Moscow in 1576 indicated in his letters how impressed he was by the splendor and glory of the robe of the Russian tsar and his crown: the ruler (he wrote) wore an imperial robe and a diadem which not even the crowns of the Spanish or French kings, nor yet the Grand Duke of Tuscany, could match. The crown of the Emperor and King of Hungary and Bohemia itself would not bear comparison. The Palace of the Muscovite ruler held so much gold and silver that one could scarcely count the plate and vessels.

Feodor Ivanovich's court (1548–1598) was no less grand or magnificent. In 1589 Ieremia, the Patriarch of Constantinople, was received by Tsaritsa Irina in a chamber "covered with the purest gold and decorated with numerous animal and bird statues made of gold and silver. The chandelier was formed in the shape of a lion with a snake in his jaws and from whose lithe body little golden candlelights hung." Bishop Arsenius, who had accompanied the patriarch, reported that the tsaritsa's magnificent robe caused him to shiver with consternation. A tiny part of this splendor would be the pride of ten emperors. Arsenius was also impressed by the rare artistry and elegance of the tsaritsa's vestments as well as "by

Parade Vestibule and Parade Stairway in Oruzheinaia Palata. ▷

274

the artistic perfection of the gold and silver tableware, which furthermore was arranged to its advantage, with moderation and feeling, on the banquet table."

The Armory is first mentioned as a workshop in the chronicles from 1547. The great fire of Moscow broke out on June 21 of that year, causing immense damage in the Kremlin and the city. The fire "completely burned the Treasury of the great tsar, the Armory with all its armor, and the Tsaritsa's Chamber housing the Tsar's wealth and the state treasury, likewise all the chamber cellars and the Imperial Stables." In addition to icons, the flames destroyed other valuable ecclesiastical objects. And after this disaster, fires and wars remained a constant plague for the Kremlin treasures. Yet the Kremlin and its palaces, cathedrals, and workshops rose anew from the ruins and ashes. Russian and international products of the art of weaponry were compiled again in the depots and storage rooms of the Armory. Moreover, after the 17th century various representative works were collected deliberately. After 1640, when the Office of Icons was abolished, the icon painters of the imperial court were assigned to the Armory. The leading Russian painters − Simon Ushakov, Feodor Zubow, Bogdan Zaltanov, Ivan Bezmin, Vasilli Poznanyski, to name only a few − decorated the chambers of the tsar and the Kremlin cathedrals with their pictures and icons, created flags and standards, and adorned Books of the Gospels with artistic covers and miniatures.

Although various types of artisans worked in the Armory, the armorers clearly had the highest rank, especially as they included the best goldsmiths, silversmiths, and jewelers. Their weapons had proved themselves in battle and were easy to handle, light, and beautiful. Thus, these weapons were considered to be the quintessence of beauty and perfection by Russian artisans. The tasteful designs − gold and silver engravings, ivory and mother-of-pearl inlays, fantastic locks in the shapes of lion's heads, dragons, dolphins, and fairy-tale monsters − made the gala weapons real works of art. International connoisseurs were also deeply impressed by the expertise of the Armory's weapon-makers. These artisans − Nikifor Kobelev, Vassili Kartsev, Ossip Alferov, Grigori Vyatkin, and Ivan Andropov − had reputations that spread far beyond the borders of Russia. Foreign master artisans were also hired for the Kremlin workshops.

The artistry of the Kremlin workshops reached its height in the second half of the 17th century. The manufactures developed into a virtual Academy of the Arts, since people who had become famous for their talents and skills as craftsmen came to Moscow from all the Russian states: Vladimir, Suzdal, Novgorod, Pskov, Murom, Yaroslavl, Kostroma, Kazan, Veliki, Ustyug, and other centers of art. They borrowed from the rich traditions of folk art,

△ A magnificent door separates the Armory collections from the Parade Vestibule.

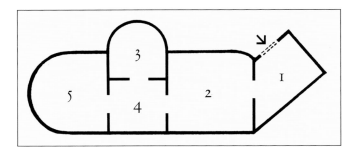

△ *Sketch of the location of the collections on the upper floor of the Armory.* 1 and 2: Gold and silver objects, jewelry. 3 and 4: Weapons, flags, and medals; products from Western Europe. 5: Gifts of silver objects from ambassadors.

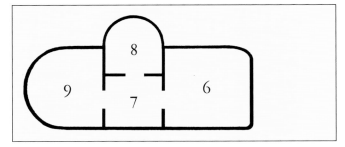

△ *Armory, sketch of the location of the collections on the ground floor.* 6: Old fabrics, embroidered work, and secular clothing from the 14th–19th century. 7: Old Russian state insignia and utensils of court ceremonies from the 13th– 19th century. 8: Horses' harnesses. 9: Coaches.

improved their skills through creative cooperation, and contributed their own, unmistakable concepts of beauty.

Peter I built a new capital on the Neva at the beginning of the 18th century. The best artisans, carpenters, and architects were called to St. Petersburg. An *ukaz* from 1711 also ordered many master armorers to the northern city. Since the gold and silver chambers had been transferred to the Armory in 1700, the production of the Kremlin workshops decreased considerably. In 1727 the Armory, the Tsaritsa's Chamber, the Grand Treasury, and the Office of Stables were merged. Thus originated the Workshop and Armory, a depot for valuable artistic and historical objects – a precursor of the present museum.

The Armory had no rooms of its own in the 18th century. Its collections were housed in the old workshops near Troitskaia Tower, in the former Grand Treasury, and in the cellars of the cathedrals and palaces. The fire of 1737 therefore caused great damage among the collections.

Not until 1808 did construction of a new building start on the site of the former Boris Godunov Court according to plans made by Ivan Vassilyevich Yegotov. The interior decoration in 1810 marked the near completion of the edifice. However, the Kremlin treasures had to be evacuated to Vizhnii-Novgorod when Napoleon's troops stood at the boundaries of Moscow in 1812. The collection was brought back to Moscow in 1814 and dispersed among seven halls of the new Yegotov building, where it remained until the mid-19th century. However, these rooms were unsuitable. For fear of fires, no heating had been installed, so that the costly articles suffered greatly from the cold and damp.

A mighty construction program was begun in the 1840s in the Moscow Kremlin. The head master architect, K. Ton, intended to integrate old Terem Palace, the cathedrals from the 15th to the 17th century, and the secular buildings into a uniform ensemble, the Grand Kremlin Palace. In 1851 the new, two-story Armory building near Borovitskii Gate was added on the site where the Office of Stables and the Granary had stood. The Armory rose steeply on Borovitskii Hill and abutted the Grand Kremlin Palace. The columns on its facade, the ornamental, double-story windows, and its combination of yellow and white harmonize superbly with the large palace ensemble.

The court was not really aware of the true value of the Armory collections, however. Many works of art were altered, given away, or recast by order of the court. Objects of no great artistic worth were added to the collections, whereas valuables often were stored on open shelves. On the other hand, progressive circles in Russia showed a keen interest in the history and fate of the Armory. Well-known scholars gained useful information here in the

△ One of the numerous restoration workshops in the Kremlin museums.

late 19th and early 20th centuries. Among other works, paintings by Ilya Yefimovich Repin, Vassili Ivanovich Zurikov, and Vladimir Yevgenjevich Makovski, as well as a sculpture by Mark Matveyevich Antokolski, reflect the inspirations given by the Armory.

The Great Revolution of October 1917 marked a new stage in Kremlin history. In January 1918, the treasures of the Kremlin were declared to be the property of the republic. When the Soviet government returned to Moscow from Petrograd (formerly St. Petersburg) and moved into the Kremlin in March 1918, Lenin assumed the sponsorship of the preservation of historical and cultural treasures as well as architectural monuments.

Since then, the exhibits in the national Armory have been carefully cared for and restored. They have doubled in number since October 1917. In 1941 during the tribulations of the war, the Kremlin treasures once again had to be removed from Moscow, but as early as May 1945 the exhibition was ready to welcome its admirers in its old home.

The new presentation more precisely accents the growth of the Kremlin workshops in the Middle Ages. The strict chronological organization provides experts and laity alike with insights into the development of many schools of art and stylistic tendencies as well as a general idea of the formation of the characteristic features of the applied arts in Russia and other countries.

Armor and Weapons

Old Russian and foreign suits of armor form the heart of the collection. The Russian division exhibits all sorts of cut-and-thrust weapons as well as the suits of armor, among which the shirts of mail are the most important.

The oldest exhibits date from the turn of the 13th century. They were parts of the battle dress belonging to Prince Yaroslav Vzevolodovich (the father of famous Alexander Nevskii) – an iron shirt of mail and a helmet decorated with engraved silver – and certainly were worn during the medieval feuds. Badly damaged by time and weathering, they were found 600 years later on the ancient site of a bloody civil war between Russian grand princes and were brought to the Armory in the 19th century.

The collection of Russian armor from the 16th and 17th centuries includes not only coats of mail – among them a unique *baidana* – but also wonderful parade suits of armor with jewels, masterful gold ornaments, imaginative engravings, and enamel decorations. Chain mail was made of thousands of small rings woven together, resulting in elastic mail shirts weighing up to 17 kilograms. Only the wealthy could afford mail shirts; they were carefully stored and passed down to succeeding generations. In the section for old Russian weapons, the bowcases and quivers will interest connoisseurs: gold and silver embroideries on leather as well as gold trimmings with enamel decorations and semiprecious stones are rare specimens.

The collection of Eastern weapons and shields is also large. Its showpiece is the 16th-century Persian shield that belonged to Prince Mztislavski: its convex surfaces are made of Damascus steel and decorated with acanthus ornaments and Eastern hunting scenes of brilliant gold incrustation. The numerous sabers, daggers, and broadswords of Damascus steel are characterized by the unusual sharpness and hardness of their blades as well as the luxurious incrustations of precious stones on their hilts and sheaths.

The Kremlin museums would be unthinkable without the Western European knights' armor from the 15th to the 17th century as well as the guns and pistols brought to Russia as gifts or display articles and stored for several centuries in the Treasury. Today they form an important addition to the museum's collections.

▷ Yaroslav Vzevolodovich's helmet from the 13th century. It was found on the banks of the Liptsia River in 1808, where a battle for the Grand Princedom of Vladimir took place in 1216. The surface of the iron skull is decorated with engraved and partially gilt silver. An inscription provides information about the helmet's ownership.

284

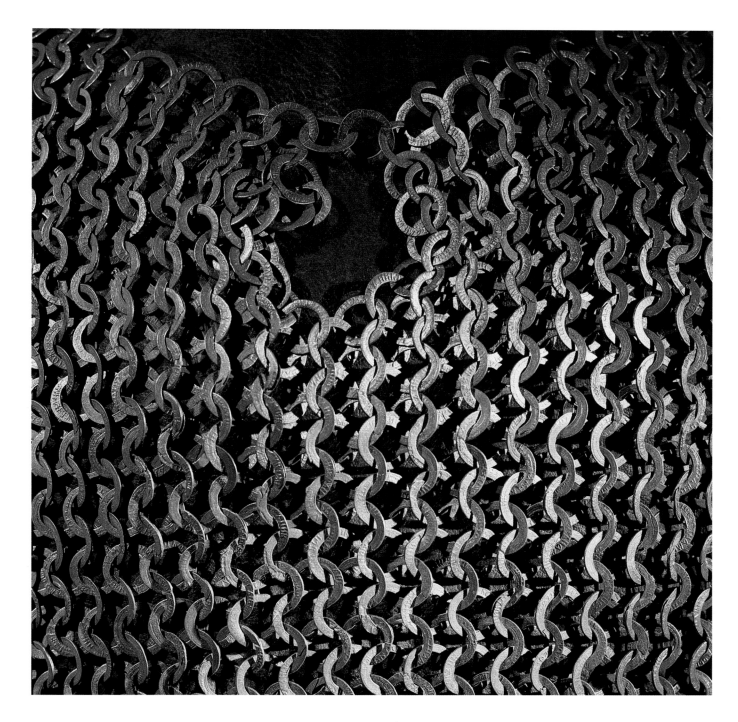

Pages 282/83: A view of the rotunda and the collection of Russian armor and weapons (upper floor, room 7 on the sketch). Above the glass cases is a frieze of portraits of Russian grand princes and tsars.

◁ Glass case containing Russian parade weapons. The picture shows some gala and hunting rifles, made in the Moscow Armory in the 17th century; wood stocks with mother-of-pearl, ivory, gold, and silver; and locks in the form of a mythical beast. Below left, Tsar Mikhail Feodorovich's Cap of Jericho, forged of Damascus steel by the Master of the Moscow Armory, Nikita Feodorovich, in 1621 and decorated with golden filigree borders in Eastern styles, pearls, rubies, and emeralds. A round badge with an enamel image of the Archangel Michael is attached to the nosepiece.

△ Boris Godunov's baidana from the 16th century. A baidana is a special variation of the usual medieval chain mail and is made of flat rings of iron, the surfaces of which are engraved and sometimes inscribed. This example bears an inscription in Old Russian: "God with us and none against us." It is the only example of a baidana in the Armory.

◁ Glass case with Near Eastern armor and weapons from the 16th and 17th centuries.

▷ Saber made by one of the most important Russian armorers, Ivan Bushuyev, from the Slatoust Weapons Factory in the Ural Mountains. The steel blade is engraved, etched, gilt, and black-finished. A battle from the Russian-Turkish War of 1827–1829 is portrayed in almost microscopic dimensions on the gold inlay work.

▽ Stocks of a rifle and a pistol with silver inlays.

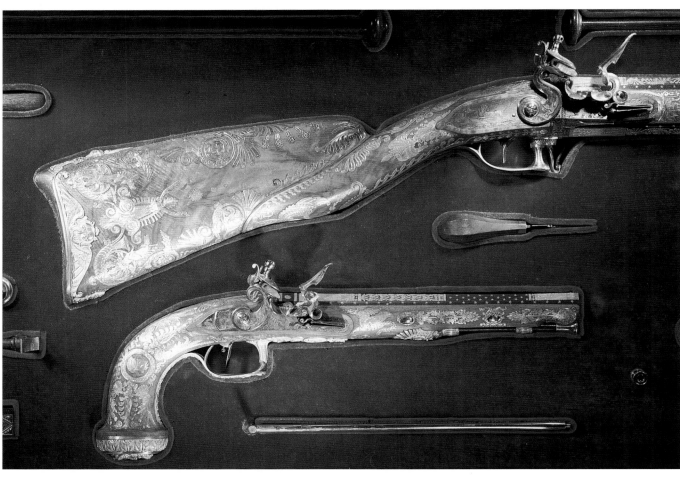

Russian Goldsmithery and Silversmithery

Known and respected the world over for its variety and comprehensiveness, the collection of Russian goldsmiths' and silversmiths' art contains several hundred exhibits from the 12th to the 17th century.

The oldest period in the history of Russian arts and crafts is represented by relatively few, yet extremely valuable, objects from the 12th to the 13th century. They include Prince Yurii Dolgorukii's famous chalice; finds from the Old Ryazan treasure discovered in 1822; princely gold jewelry, usually in a filigree technique and decorated with cloisonné enamel and gems; and an embossed chalice of the Prince of Chernigov. Characteristically enough, these are products of the various centers of arts and crafts of ancient Rus, during the period when several small feudal princedoms were competing with one another. This was not the least important reason for the formation of independent schools, each with unmistakable aesthetic styles and craftmanship.

The Russian princedoms were not completely united under Moscow until the turn of the 16th century. The process of unification culminated in the liberation from the Tatar yoke and a considerable upswing in Russian art and culture, with Moscow at its center. The Kremlin workshops also became the leading jewelry-makers during the 16th century. The best goldsmiths and silversmiths flocked to Moscow from throughout the country. Their individual styles and traditions merged into a variegated art trend that came to be known as the Moscow School.

Products of the Moscow School comprise the heart of the gold and silver collection in the Armory. Relatively little remains from the 15th century. The filigree covers for the Gospels made for Uspenskii Cathedral are particularly noteworthy; their simple overall design contrasts and harmonizes perfectly with the rather bizarre, yet superb, ornamentation. The handwritten texts are impressive for their elegant, courtly calligraphy, their exquisite color combinations, and their magnificent vignette decorations.

▷ Gilt memorial stones for Tsarevitch Dmitrii and for Kirill of Belozersk.

Pages 290/91: Large exhibition hall on the upper floor with glass cases containing Russian gold and silver products.

△ Folding icon for Ivan Gryasev, a civil servant, created by a master artisan of the Armory in the 17th century. The combination of the painted icon and the encasement decorated with pearls and gems is particularly striking.

◁ Diptych from Moscow, 1589.

▷ Gilt reliquary in the shape of a six-sided domed building with arcades and columns. Chased floral ornamentation adorns the walls. Two holy warriors stand guard on the double-winged portal.

293

«РЯЗАНСКИЙ КЛАД»
РЯЗАНЬ, XII в.
Золото, драгоценные камни,
жемчуг, эмаль, скань.

△ Chalice made by a master artisan from the Moscow
Armory in 1664. A present from the boyarina Anna Moro-
sova to the Chudov Monastery in memory of her husband.

◁ Glass case containing the oldest Russian gold and silver
work in the Moscow Kremlin. Found in Staraya Ryazan,
in 1822. Objects date from about the end of the 12th to the
beginning of the 13th century. Splendid jewelry (earrings,
collars, bracelets, rings, etc.) of gold and enamel.

△ Star-shaped golden earring. Made in Kiev in the 12th century.

▷ Forehead decoration of gilt silver from Ryazan.

▷ Cover of a Book of Gospels, created by a Russian master craftsman in 1568 according to the 14th-century tradition. Gilt silver filigree and tiny cast figures.

◁ Cover of a Book of Gospels, made by a master artisan from the Armory in 1571. Gift of Ivan the Terrible to the Cathedral of the Annunciation. It displays a classic division of area, with four medallions depicting the evangelists in the corners.

▽ Two covers of the Gospels from the workshops in the Moscow Kremlin. They are superb examples of the colorful Muscovite art of enameling. At the left, gift of Tsar Feodor Alexeyevich to the Church of the Crucifixion, made in 1681. At the right; gift of the same tsar to the Church of the Resurrection, created in 1678.

298

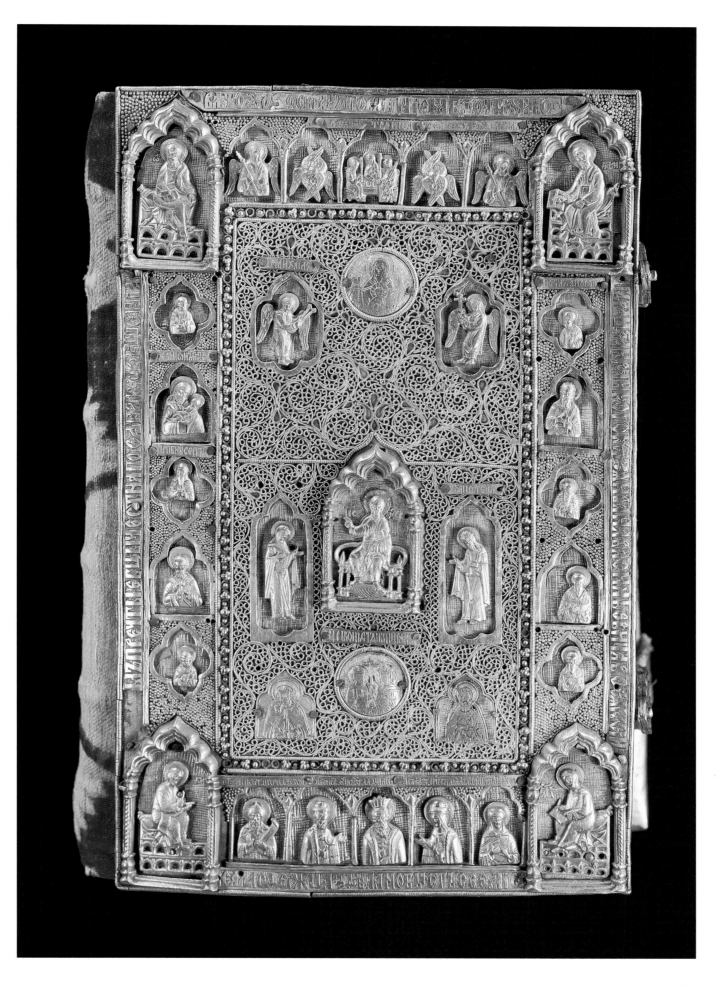

The 16th century is represented quite comprehensively and in variety. The characteristic features of the goldsmithery and silversmithery of that time are refined, splendid designs, skillful compositions, and the use of polychrome decoration. A particularly interesting technique is the use of enamel overlay work on filigree backgrounds. The art of niello resulted in real masterpieces of engraving, chief among them the golden censer (from 1598) that Irina Godunova presented to the Cathedral of the Archangel. Its extremely delicate black ornaments and the graceful figures of the saints appear to be finely drawn in ink, whereas the large, round, costly sapphires and topazes lend the censer its majestic ceremoniousness.

The sumptuousness of these 16th-century articles can be attributed to their having been produced in the Kremlin workshops on special order of the tsar or members of his family. Most of them have considerable weight, are made of gold, and are heavily encrusted with gems and pearls. Among them are Ivan Grozny's (the Terrible's) Gospels from 1571, his bosom cross, Irina Godunova's chalice from 1598, and icon encasings. The golden bowl made in 1561 that was given by Ivan Grozny as a wedding present to his second wife, Maria Temrykovna, weighs 3.6 kilograms.

Light-hearted, luxurious decorations with bright fairytale motifs marked the 17th century arts and crafts. The numerous and colorful enameled, bejeweled, and engraved ornaments suited this trend especially well, which became distinctive in the second half of the 17th century. Frequently, so many gems were used that the beauty of any particular emerald or ruby could no longer be discerned. They were intended solely as a means of adding color to an ornament, although the artisans sometimes set exceptionally large stones. The "Vladimir Mother of God" icon contains two emeralds weighing 100 carats each.

Color schemes combining green, red, yellow, and brownish-violet were preferred. They provided brilliant contrasts to the white pearls applied to icons and gala clothing in extravagant numbers.

Other centers of arts and crafts are represented in the Armory in addition to the Kremlin workshops, to which they are hardly inferior in terms of splendor and artistic expertise. Several distinct schools of jewel-making can be recognized. However, the art of enameling from the northern Russian city Zolvechigodsk belongs to a class of its own. It is known as "Usol'e enameling" in the history of Russian art. The objects in the Armory are superb early 17th-century examples of Russian enameling, which reached its height in the 18th century.

A cross made by a Russian master craftsman in 1562. Embossed gold with pearls and gems. ▷

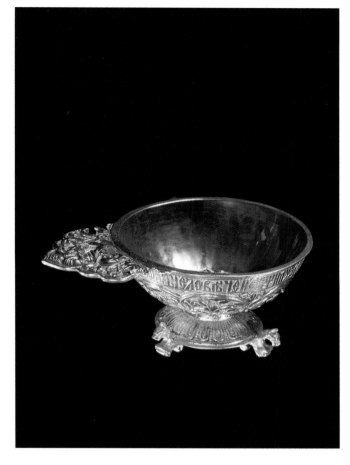

◁ Cover for the Gospels made in 1603 of gilt silver, gems, and pearls.

▷ Drinking cup made of gold in Moscow in the 17th century.

▷ ▽ Spherical drinking vessel (*bratina*) of the civil servant Ivan Gramotin, made by a Russian master craftsman in the first third of the 17th century. Made of gilt silver, it bears an engraved inscription with the name of the orderer.

▽ Drinking vessel, produced in Moscow at the end of the 16th century.

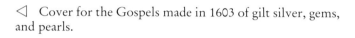

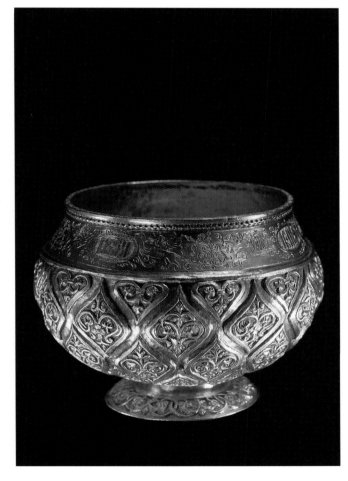

△ Silver mug, made in the first half of the 17th century in Moscow.

◁ "Trinity" icon. Encasing from 1676–1682, made by masters from the Armory. The bright shades of enamel have been cast in flowing shapes and combined with jewels – a typical design for the Armory craftsmen of that period.

Rare specimens among the exhibits from the late 18th and early 19th centuries include articles embellished in niello that were made in Tobolsk, Veliki Ustyug, and Vologda. Moscow and St. Petersburg were the leading centers of gold and silver work during that period. Two schools developed in this art: the more severe, Europeanized style of the northern city and the somewhat freer tradition of the old capital, which drew on Russian traditions. New customs were in fashion and led to the great popularity of samovars (Russian tea kettles heated with wood), tea and coffee pots, and whole sets of tableware. Silver statues were especially valued. Catherine II even had children's tea sets made by well-known master artisans from St. Petersburg. Display articles were frequently embellished with picturesque enamel decorations and jewels of light and pastel shades, a style of adornment especially popular in the second half of the 18th century. Often, an object is so heavily encrusted with diamonds, aquamarines, and amethysts that the article itself can hardly be seen underneath. G. Unger, one of the most renowned master artisans from St. Petersburg, set 3,500 diamonds, aquamarines, and amethysts in a rhomboid-shaped net design on the cover of a book of Gospels.

In the early 19th century, laurel and oak leaves became popular symbols of victory and ornamental shapes in reaction to the events of 1812. Examples include the overly large chased and gilt bowls that belonged to one of the heros of the Patriotic War of 1812, the Cossack ataman M. Platov.

Special mention is due the highly admired collection of jewelry and toys from the house of Fabergé, the imperial jewelers of the late 19th and early 20th centuries. Most of the examples are small luxury items made of gold and adorned with gems, decorative stones, and enamel work. All Fabergé products are marked by their absolute precision and excellent workmanship. Among other collections, the Moscow Armory owns the largest exhibition of Fabergé Easter egg toys. The Fabergé jewelers rediscovered the semiprecious stones from the Ural Mountains, which they used when designing humorous small statues in the manner of conversation pieces.

▷ The Armory houses an interesting collection of enamel work from the various centers of jewel-making. Pictured here are a silver jewelry casket and a drinking vessel from Zolvechigodsk created near the end of the 17th century. The five medallions on the inside surface of the vessel depict personifications of the five human senses: smell; taste; at the bottom, sight; at the left, hearing; and in the middle, touch. The Usol'e enamel work as is shown on the casket, displays a new combination of ornaments and realistic portrayals of plants and animals.

307

МОДЕЛЬ КРЕЙСЕРА «ПАМЯТЬ АЗОВА»
В ЯЙЦЕ ИЗ ГЕЛИОТРОПА

ПЕТЕРБУРГ, 1891 г. ФИРМА ФАБЕРЖЕ.
МАСТЕР МИХАИЛ ПЕРХИН

Products from the house of Fabergé. Gustave Fabergé of Lyons founded a workshop-store in St. Petersburg in 1842. He opened new branches in 1887 in Moscow, in 1890 in Odessa, in 1903 in London, and in 1905 in Kiev. The company was famous at the beginning of the 20th century and at one time employed 500 experts. *Above:* a model of the "Pamyat Azova" cross of gold and platinum. *Facing page:* a golden clock with a white hour band and an immovable hand made of diamonds by M. Perkhin in 1899.

Gifts of Silver from Foreign Envoys

The Armory's collection of Western European silver artwork embraces over 1,000 exhibits from many different countries, making it the largest in the world. The greater part of the collection consists of gifts from foreign governments brought by envoys from various European states in the 16th and 17th centuries. These costly objects bear witness to bygone diplomacy and in their own way throw light on the development of the relations between the Russian state and England, Holland, Sweden, Denmark, Poland, and the Holy Roman Empire. Many of the pieces bear inscriptions in Old Russian indicating the time and place of manufacture. These inscriptions are verified by the inventories of the tsar's treasures from the 17th century, which are now carefully stored in the National Archives for old documents in Moscow.

No other museum in the world owns such a large, comprehensive collection of English silverware from the late 16th and first half of the 17th century. From 1558 to 1664, the emissaries of Queen Elizabeth I, King James I, King Charles I, and King Charles II presented valuable gifts to the Russian tsars Ivan the Terrible, Boris Godunov, Mikhail Romanov, and Alexei Mikhailovich. The oldest piece, a cup dating from 1557 or 1558, is remarkably similar to a silver drinking vessel signed by Hans Holbein the Younger (the German painter is known to have stayed at the court of Henry IV in London). Among numerous other exceptional works of art, the silver wine vessels shaped like snow leopards and weighing approximately 30 kilograms each are considered to be particularly valuable. The cups, bowls, and candlesticks in the collection are characterized by their considerable size, muted lines, and massive ornaments.

▷ Glass cases containing gifts of English silverware. The case at the left holds one of the famous snow leopards that sit and bear shields in their front paws. The hollow figure served as a wine vessel; the removable head was the cover. Of cast and hammer forged silver, it was made in London in 1600–1601. The figure was brought to Moscow in 1629 by the English merchant Fabian Ulyanov.

Chief among the other European styles represented in the Armory are those of the Dutch, in products from Amsterdam; the Swedish, in Stockholm silver; and the French, in works by Parisian jewelers. However, German silver from the 16th and 17th centuries undoubtedly forms the most significant part of the collection. It is also the world's largest such collection, comprised of gifts brought by envoys and merchants to Moscow from Sweden, Denmark, Poland, and Austria. The size of the Armory collection affords a good glimpse into regional stylistic differences and leading centers of this craft (Augsburg, Nuremberg, and Hamburg, among others), as well as a fair idea of the work and "hand" of many important master silversmiths. Whole sections in the Armory are devoted to names such as Yamnitzer, Petzolt, and the Ritter and Fischer families from Nuremberg, and Jakob Mores, Lambrecht, and Richels from Hamburg. The collection of products from the Augsburg school alone numbers over 450 works from the most renowned artists, including Epfenhauser, Glaubich, Fries, Drentwett, Gelb, Manlich, Biller, and Thelot.

▷ Gilt silver saltcellar made in Hamburg about 1635–1644.

Page 314: The collection of German diplomatic silver contains numerous table decorations such as this celestial globe from Hamburg, created about 1649–1655.

Page 315: Decorative sculpture in the shape of a stag. Made of gilt silver in Hamburg between approximately 1635 and 1644.

312

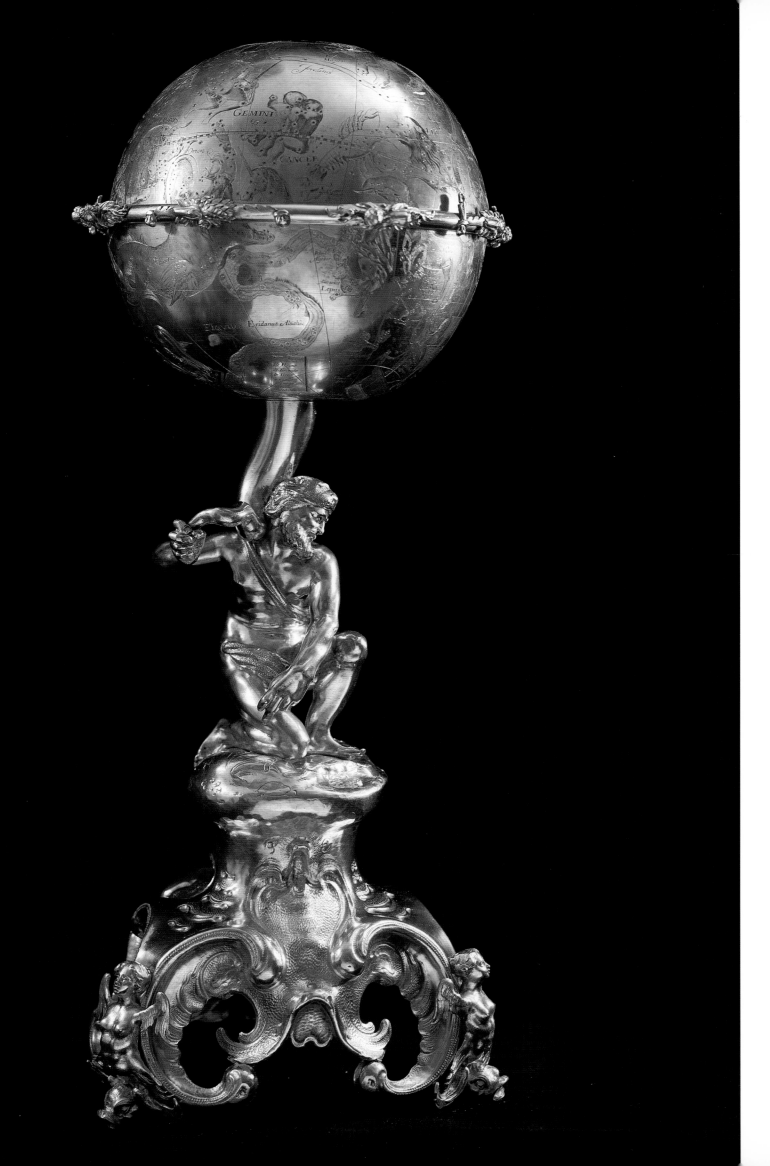

◁ ◁ Silver cup from Nuremberg dating from 1541.

◁ Silver double cup from Hamburg, from the end of the 18th or beginning of the 19th century.

▽ Detail from a Hamburg double cup. The singer Orpheus is depicted charming the animals with his music.

▷ Silver candlestick from Hamburg, created about 1649–1655.

△ Glass case displaying gifts from Poland, mainly from the 17th century. Some of them were created by German artists.

◁ Crucifix from Limoges dating from the 13th century. Cast copper with enamel and pearls.

Works by Persian and Turkish goldsmiths from the 16th and 17th centuries account for a substantial part of the collection of diplomats' gifts. During the 17th century, the Constantinople school was marked by strong, richly colored enamel and the generous use of precious stones. Tsaritsa Natalya Kirillovna's two massive bowls are especially noteworthy: countless rubies, emeralds, and diamonds form floral designs on a green enamel background. The fine dishes, combs, fans, and perfume jars made from cut glass and jade are also embellished with floral ornaments of small rubies, emeralds, and thin, encrusted gold wires.

▷ Steel helmet made in Persia, gilt and encrusted with precious stones. It is shown here in a studio in the Kremlin restoration workshops.

Robes and Fabrics

The collection of robes and fabrics in the Treasury is renowned throughout the world; many of the exhibits are directly connected to historical events or personages. Until 1919, the majority of these valuables were kept in the Patriarchal Sacristy, the sacristies of the Moscow Kremlin's cathedrals and monasteries, and the numerous churches. The oldest robes date from the 14th and 15th centuries; two sakkos of Byzantine satin that belonged to Metropolitan Peter and Metropolitan Photii Metropolitan Peter's sakkos dates from 1322 and is made of light blue satin with woven stripes of gold and edged crosses resulting in a severe, elegant beauty. The large and the small sakkos of Metropolitan Photii are completely covered with designs woven into the fabric. The Muscovite Metropolitan Peter is portrayed on the small sakkos and on the large robe Vasilii II, Grand Prince of Moscow; his wife, Sophia Vitautovna; their daughter Anna; her husband, the future Emperor of Byzantium, John Palaeologus; as well as Photii himself. The collection of Byzantine textiles bears witness not only to the political and cultural relations of Russia with Byzantium, but also to the spreading reputation of the Muscovite grand princes. Furthermore, these fabrics can be considered artworks of an unequalled craftmanship and decorative perfection.

Persian and Turkish fabrics represent the early Near Eastern schools in the collection. The Persian textiles are characterized by discreet colors: pink, light blue, dark blue, green and brown, and delicate foliage, scroll and meander motifs: light-hearted designs in which carnations, tulips, lilies and hyacinths most frequently appear. Persian fabric patterns often also portray human and animal figures. The Persian textiles, including brocades, velvets, and silk cloths, are expecially valued for their patterns and tasteful color combinations. On the other hand, Turkish fabrics from the 17th century feature strong color contrasts and large designs, the favorites being flowers of the pomegranate tree and carnations in pointed ovals. Turkish artists avoided portrayals of living beings. Bright red and wine red combined with light and dark blue or green were the preferred color combinations.

▷ Sakkos of Patriarch Nikon. An Italian product of satin, taffeta, and velvet set with gold and silver embroideries, pearls, and jewels, from the 17th century.

322

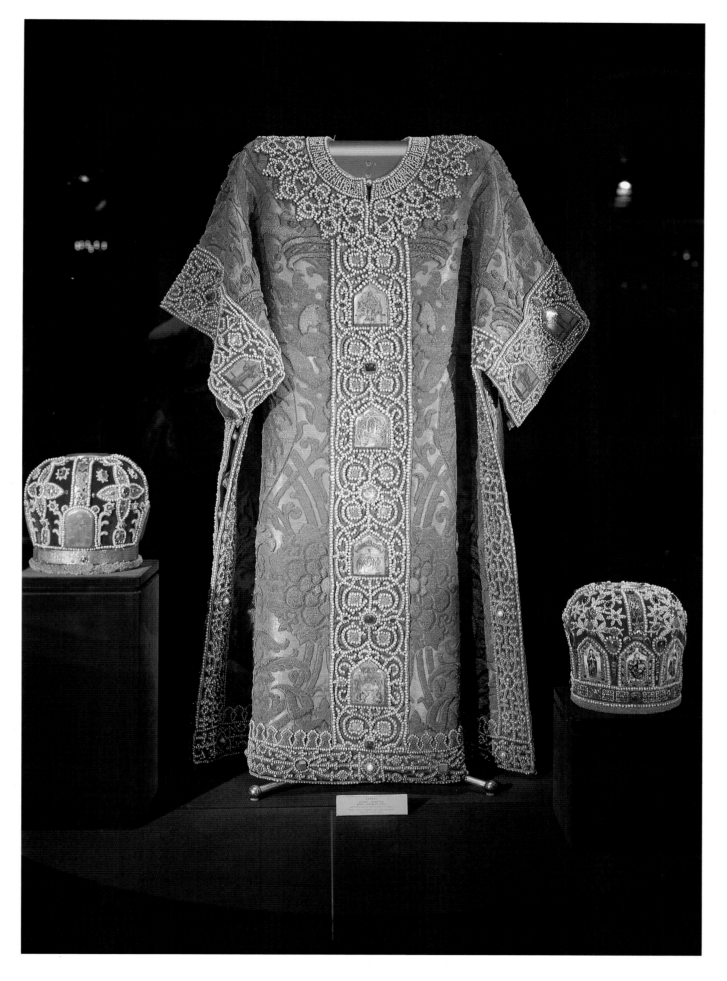

Italian fabrics were held in high regard in the 16th and 17th centuries: velvet, silk with large patterns, and *alto ebasso* (a fabric of two different heights of nap). These textiles, interwoven with gold and silver threads, remind one of wrought metals. Splendid and elegant relief designs of beautiful shapes are formed by combining gold wire eyelets and appliqué patterns. During the 17th century, silks were in great demand at the tsarist and patriarchal courts. No other textiles would do for the robes of the tsars, boyars, and high clergymen. In the Kremlin workshops in 1654, Patriarch Nikon's sakkos was sewn of silk with foliate and scroll ornaments. It weighed 24 kilograms, 16 of which were contributed by precious stones and pearls attached to the shoulders, sleeves, shirtfront, and hems.

Around the mid-17th century, the expensive, heavy Italian textiles were replaced on the world market by light French fabrics, chiefly from Lyons. These cloths were marked by daring color combinations and peculiar patterns. In the 1630s a velvet workshop arose in Moscow, located on the bank of the Moskva between Tainitskaia Tower and the Water Tower. However, luxurious fabrics were not produced en masse in Russia until the 18th century. Russian silk cornered a leading position on the international market in the 19th century.

The collection of secular clothing from the 16th to the 18th century includes wonderful specimens of Old Russian national costumes with their diverse cuts and decorations, as well as official robes worn by the tsars for coronations and receptions for foreign envoys. These usually were heavily studded with gems and pearls. Peter I's clothing is especially interesting, since he wore both national costumes and European clothes. In the 18th century, Western European fashions became increasingly prevalent among the Russian upper class. The coronation robes of Catherine I, Anna Ivanovna, Yelizaveta Petrovna (1742), and Catherine II (1745) give an idea of fashions at the Russian court. The 19th-century silver brocade dresses that belonged to the Russian empresses are prime examples of the so-called Pseudo-Russian style. Men's clothing is represented in the Armory by, among other things, gala uniforms for coronations and diplomatic receptions from the 18th and 19th centuries.

▷ Detail from the sakkos of Metropolitan Alexei from 1364, showing cross-stitching and appliquéd metal plaquets with enamel. The stole for the sakkos has also been preserved.

▷ ▽ Stole with pearl embroidery and chasuble of velvet and interwoven gold, both from the 17th century. The chasuble is Italian.

▽ View of the glass case containing the sakkos of Metropolitan Alexei from 1364.

△ In the background, on the left, the famous sakkos of Metropolitan Peter from 1322, one of the oldest pieces of clothing in the Armory. It displays a harmonic pattern of interwoven gold and silver threads and blue silk. In the foreground, the chasuble of Metropolitan Photii from the 15th century. The robe is almost completely covered with gold and silver embroideries. Byzantine work.

▷ State robe of Peter I from the 17th century. Venetian gold brocade with silver designs. The *barma* (regalia collar), from the Golden Tsaritsa Chamber, was made by a Russian artisan.

Page 328: View of part of the Hall of Robes on the ground floor.

Page 329: Lady's boots from the 17th century. Pearls had always been a favorite decoration for Russian clothing and were first mentioned in this context in a chronicle from the 10th century. Only the rich could afford pearl decorations. The art of embroidering with pearls was practiced not only at the courts of the boyars and tsars, but also in monasteries and on large farms. Russia once possessed rich sources of pearls in its northern rivers larger and more beautiful than those from the seas.

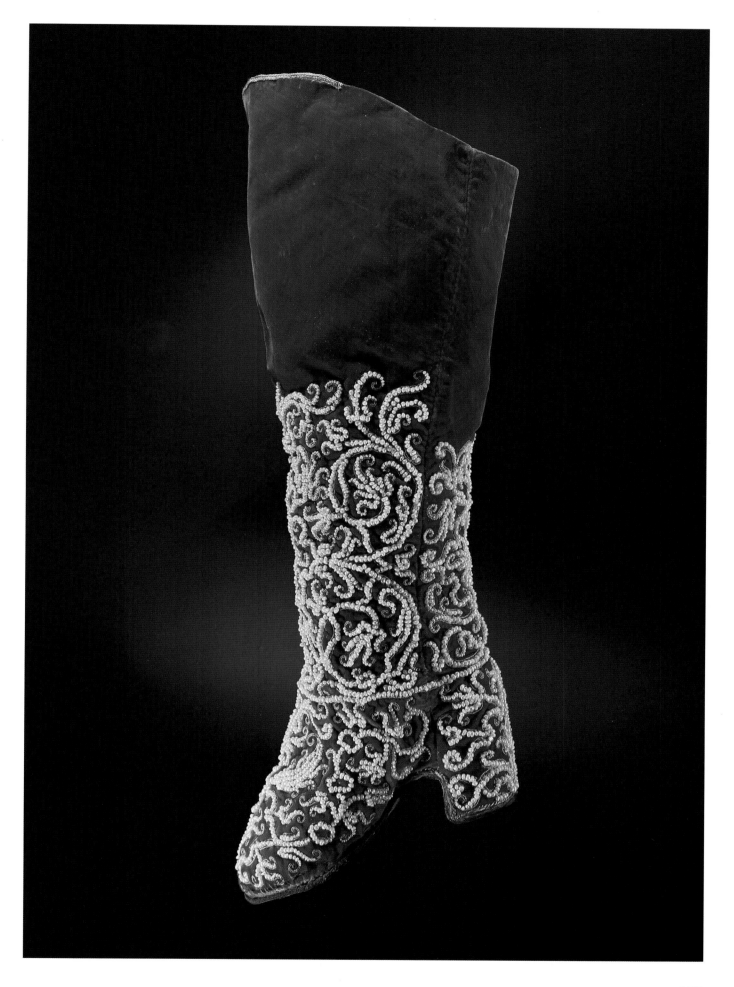

Regalia and Court Carriages

The collection of old regalia can only be termed extraordinary. The actual symbols of power and status form the heart of the collection: crowns, scepters, imperial orbs, and thrones from the former Treasury of the Tsar – all essential utensils for the solemn ceremonies at the court. The cap-shaped Russian crowns are usually lined and edged with exquisite black sable fur. Legends surround the hereditary crown of the Russian tsars, the extremely valuable crown of Monomakh from the 13th or 14th century. Highlights of Old Russian jewel-making include the crowns of Ivan the Terrible, Mikhail Romanov, and Peter I. Yet even amongst such illustrious surroundings, the insignia of the Grand Regalia still appear magnificent. Kremlin artisans made them for Mikhail Feodorovich in 1627 and 1628. The Grand Regalia are comprised of the crown, scepter, imperial orb, and quiver. All of these objects are studded with many astonishingly high-carat sapphires, emeralds, and diamonds, as well as pearls and colored enamels. The Kremlin workshops also produced the diamond crowns for the twin brothers Ivan and Peter in 1682, each of which was set with a thousand diamonds of different sizes. Other treasures in the collection are the earliest European-style imperial thrones, the first of which was created for the coronation of Catherine I, the wife of Peter I. Empress Anna's crown, with over 2,500 diamonds, is regarded as the most valuable.

Superior material, exquisite craftsmanship, and a wealth of gems mark the collection of thrones, the oldest of which belonged to Ivan the Terrible. This 16th-century Western European work is covered with ivory plates fantastically carved to depict mythological and Biblical motifs and scenes. The throne was partially restored as early as the 17th century by Russian artisans. The Iranian thrones are of great worth, both historically and in terms of materials. One of them, a present of Shah Abbaz I to Boris Godunov in 1604, displays a fairy-tale splendor. It is covered with gold leaf and studded with tourmaline and turquoise. Alexei Mikhailovich's diamond throne from 1659 is encased by gold and silver sheets with stamped and openwork filigree decorations and edgings of superb Persian miniatures and nearly a thousand diamonds.

△ Items from the glass case containing state crowns. In front, the Oriental Cap of Monomakh from the late 13th or early 14th century, last used in a coronation of a tsar in 1682. At the upper left, the crown of Empress Anna Ivanovna, made in St. Petersburg in 1730. At the upper right, the Kazaner Cap of Ivan the Terrible, made in the workshops of the Moscow Kremlin in 1553.

◁ Grand Regalia of Tsar Mikhail Feodorovich: crown, scepter, and imperial orb. Created in the Kremlin in 1627–1628.

▽ Detail of the imperial orb in the Grand Regalia. Enamel miniature depicting David's victory over Goliath.

▷ Detail from the scepter of the Grand Regalia.

△ The large imperial crown was produced by J. Pozier for the coronation of Catherine II in 1762. It is made of silver, diamonds, pearls, and spinels (a pink to purple-red variety of ruby) by Jeremia Pozier, the tsar's court jeweler. The crown was designed in the traditional form of two semispheres; a clasp with a ball and cross curves between them. The diamonds are set in the shape of laurel leaves, symbols of power and renown. The crown is kept in the Diamond Fund.

▷ Catherine I's throne. Gilt wooden frame, velvet upholstery with appliquéd gold and silver embroideries.

Pages 336/37: At left, throne of Tsar Boris Godunov, made in Persia at the end of the 16th century. Gift of Shah Abbaz I to the tsar in 1605. At right, throne of Ivan the Terrible, made in Western Europe at the end of the 16th century. Fantastic ivory carvings on a wooden frame.

335

The collection of riding equipment for imperial processions has been connected to the regalia. The Russian imperial court considered these ceremonies to be very important. This led to the establishment of the Office of Stables, which was responsible for the manufacture and servicing of the gala carriages and harnesses as well as the organization of ceremonial pageants. The Office of Stables employed first-rate artisans, including the silversmiths and jewelers who made costly harnesses, saddles, stirrups, bridles, and other riding equipment, as well as the horse blankets and caparisons, that form the present collection. An abundance of such equipment was required, for a hundred or more horses in gala array were harnessed in front of the tsar's carriage during a procession.

The breathtaking opulence of the gold, silver, precious stones, and pearls was intended to emphasize the significance of the processions. The honor of leading the court horses fell exclusively to the highest nobility, the boyars. It is thus quite understandable that the boyars wore festive, precious robes on those occasions. Thousands of silver bells and chains of bells created a backdrop of sound eminently suited to the colorful, enchanting show for the tsar's obedient, enthusiastic subjects.

In addition to the Russian objects, mostly made in the Kremlin workshops, the collection of riding equipment includes objects from Turkey, Iran, Central Asia, and China, where horses traditionally were honored and decked out in splendor. The rather small collection of Western European saddles and horse blankets from the 17th and 18th centuries features gold and silver patterns woven into the fabric. National traditions, forms, and patterns can be clearly distinguished.

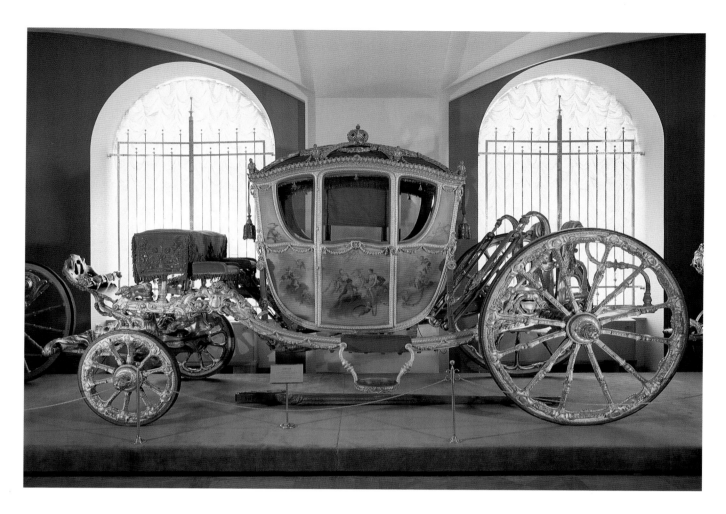

△ Catherine II's parade carriage, made in England in the 18th century. Gorgeously painted by an artist from the circleof Watteau.

◁ Gilt silver pair of stirrups made in Moscow in the 17th century. Part of a gala harness. The tsar's coat of arms is engraved in the middle of the flat surface.

▷ View of a row of carriages. The Armory possesses an unusually comprehensive collection of coaches from the 16th to the 18th century.

Equipages are on display in one of the halls on the ground floor, illustrating the development of carriage building and styles of decoration in Russia and other countries from the 16th through the 18th century. Although some of the carriages came from foreign countries, most of the present exhibits were produced in the workshops of the Office of Stables by Russian smiths and by master carriage-makers and saddlers. Two large workshops had been founded in Moscow and St. Petersburg by the 18th century, so that carriage imports decreased substantially, consisting solely of magnificent parade equipages produced on special commission for outstanding occasions.

The oldest carriage in the collection, a present from Queen Elizabeth for Boris Godunov, is English and dates from around 1600. The vehicle's size and weight are impressive. Because the body has no springs, but is hung on leather straps, it probably afforded its passengers little comfort. There is no box, so the driver either had to run alongside the carriage and lead the horse by the reins or ride. The axles do not revolve; therefore, servants had to lift the back wheels in curves. The coach's interior, lined with Persian velvet, was hidden from curious glances by heavy curtains. The exterior was lavishly adorned with such works as skillfully executed carvings depicting a victory parade and a hunting scene. This one-horse carriage was certainly a technical masterpiece in its time. It was also favored by Boris Godunov's successors throughout the 17th century. Another notable exhibit is the carriage made by the French master artisan Bournihall in 1757, which Count K. Razumovski gave Empress Yelizaveta Petrovna. No less a painter than François Boucher painted the walls and doors with heady Rococo scenes. The carriage has not required restoration to this day.

In the 18th and 19th centuries, a carriage built by the Berlin master artisan Johann Hoppenhaupt in 1746 formed the attraction of many processions. Eight horses drew this coupe, which, although pompously decorated with Rococo laurel leaves, Renaissance scrolling, rocaille, and bands of scrollwork, still appeared light and graceful.

△ Children's carriage.

▽ Carriage of Empress Anna Ivanovna from St. Petersburg, 1739.

△ Saddle covered with gold foil, to which wire cloisonné (the areas of enamel are lined by twisted gold or silver wires) has been applied. Made by master artisans from the Armory in 1682.

▷ Parade horse bearing a richly decorated halter.

344

The Diamond Fund of the USSR

The exhibition "Diamond Fund of the USSR" opened on the lower floor of the Armory in 1967. It has since gained world renown as a collection of precious stones and jewelry unequaled in wealth and of considerable artistic value. A national depot for particularly costly pieces had been established as early as 1920, which was expanded to incorporate the administration of the former Russian crown jewels in 1922. This basic collection was enriched over the next decades by significant treasures of jewelry: extraordinarily large precious stones, world-famous gold and platinum nuggets, and singularly beautiful semi-precious stones from the Ural mountains.

The value of the diamonds has increased with the passing of the 20th century. Turbulent industrial development and scientific and technological revolutions have made the diamond the symbol of progress. In the Soviet Union, the search for and exploitation of diamond reserves were carried out under extremely difficult climatic conditions. In Yakutia, in the middle of the Taiga, arose the Soviet center of diamonds, Mirny. Huge diamonds were discovered there and eloquently named Voz'chod or Valentina Tereshkova for the period of the first space flights, or Vilyuski or Komsomolski in honor of the young explorers of the Taiga.

△ ▷ Medal of the Order of St. Andrew, made of silver and diamonds around 1795–1800. The most important emblems of this order, which was founded by Peter I in 1698, are a St. Andrew's cross bearing the martyr nailed to the cross and a star worn on the left of the chest. The star shown here, which is part of the tsar's chain and completely encrusted with brilliants, stands out among the numerous star-shaped orders in the Diamond Fund.

▷ Glass case displaying Russian precious and semi-precious stones. The lapidary craft was rapidly perfected in Russia after Peter I had a stone polishing workshop set up in Petershof, near St. Petersburg, in 1725.

Many legends revolve around "Orloff" (189.62 carats), which has adorned the Russian imperial scepter since 1774. Discovered in India at the beginning of the 17th century, it first decorated an idol in Serenghan. It was stolen from the temple by a French soldier at the beginning of the 18th century; came into possession of the Persian Shah Nadir, who sold it to a rich merchant; then again belonged to a soldier, until it was bought by Count G. Orlov for 400,000 rubles and given to Empress Catherine II in the 1770s.

The history of the "Shah" diamond is no less romantic. Faultlessly transparent, shimmering yellowish-red, it was discovered in the 16th century and belonged to the ruler of the Indian province Ahmednagar, as the first inscription dating from 1591 claims. During the period of brutal, bloody feuds, the gem came into possession of the dynasty of the Grand Moguls, as recorded in the second inscription. Later, according to the third inscription from 1824, it belonged to the Persian Shah Nadir. After the Russian envoy and excellent author A. Griboyedov was murdered during anti-Russian riots in Teheran, the "Shah" was given to the Russian tsar Nicholas I.

The olive-green chrysolite (192.6 carats) found on the volcanic island Zeberget in the Red Sea is another of the Fund's precious stones with an eventful history. The Grand Imperial Crown, made in 1762 by the Russian court jeweler Jeremia Pozier for the coronation of Catherine II, must certainly be considered one of the most spectacular treasures on exhibit. The world's largest spinel (398.72 carats) reigns among the opulent diamonds and pearls in this fantastic work of jewelry.

The collection of platinum and gold nuggets contains stones of unusual quality and shape, to which the names of the nuggets correspond: for example, "The Large Triangle" (36 kilograms) and "The Grand Thousand" (14 kilograms), or the stones in beautiful natural shapes that spark the imagination – "Mephisto," "Hare's Ear," "Horsehead," and "Camel." This unique collection is completed by a section displaying especially magnificent emeralds, sapphires, topazes, amethysts, and other precious stones.

△ The largest collection of medals from Russian orders is owned by the Diamond Fund. Many of them formerly belonged to the tsar's family, including the Order of the Golden Fleece shown above. It is made of gold, burnt Brazilian topazes, and diamonds and originated in Spain around the middle of the 19th century.

APPENDICES

List of Artists

Suggested reading

This is a list of works selected from the wide range of literature on the Kremlin, most of which has appeared in Russian. The list is arranged in chronological order.

Ageyev: CATALOGUE OF ATTRACTIONS OF THE KREMLIN PALACE. Moscow 1865.

Fabrizius, P.: THE KREMLIN IN MOSCOW. Moscow 1883.

INVENTORY OF THE ARMORY. Parts 1–7. Moscow 1884–93.

Istomin, G.: LIST OF SHRINES AND ATTRACTIONS IN THE MOSCOW USPENSKII CATHEDRAL (OF THE ASSUMPTION). Moscow 1888.

Platonov: THE ARMORY IN MOSCOW. In: BIBLIOGRAPHER 1890.

Zabelin, N.Y.: HISTORY OF THE CITY OF MOSCOW. 2nd ed. Moscow 1905.

MOSCOW'S PAST AND PRESENT. Vols. 1–12. Moscow 1909–12.

Bartenov, S.P.: THE MOSCOW KREMLIN OF OLD AND TODAY. Moscow 1912–16.

DOCUMENTS OF THE GREAT PROLETARIAN REVOLUTION. Vol. 2. Moscow 1948.

Zytin, P.V.: HISTORY OF THE PLANNING AND BUILDING OF MOSCOW. Vol. 1. Moscow 1950–52.

Birzite, L.: DEVELOPMENT OF NATIONAL FORMS OF ARCHITECTURE IN THE MOSCOW KREMLIN. Riga 1954.

THE NATIONAL ARMORY IN THE MOSCOW KREMLIN. Scientific Essays. Moscow 1954.

HISTORY OF RUSSIAN ARCHITECTURE. Moscow 1956.

HISTORY OF MOSCOW. VOL. 6, PART I. MOSCOW 1957.

DECREES OF THE SOVIET GOVERNMENT. Vol. 1, Moscow 1957; Vol. 2, 1959.

MEMORIES OF VLADIMIR ILYICH LENIN. Vol. 2, Moscow 1957; Vols. 1–4, 1961–70.

Gontsharova, A., and N. Gordeyev: THE KREMLIN TOWER CLOCK. Moscow 1959.

Andreyev, A., B. Pankov, and Ye. Smirnova: LENIN IN THE KREMLIN. Moscow 1960.

Voronin, I.K.: THE ARCHITECTURE OF NORTHEAST RUSSIA IN THE 12TH–15TH CENTURIES. Vol. 2. Moscow 1962.

Snegiryov, V.L.: ARCHITECT BAZHENOV. Moscow 1962.

Mikhailov, A.K.: THE BELFRY OF IVAN THE GREAT IN MOSCOW. Moscow 1963.

ON THE HISTORY OF THE DEVELOPMENT OF SOVIET CULTURE, 1917–1918. Moscow 1964.

THE ARMORY. Moscow 1964.

Rabinovich, M.G.: ABOUT OLD AND NEW MOSCOW. Moscow 1964.

Possokhin, M., A. Midoyants, and N. Pekareva: THE PALACE OF CONGRESS IN THE KREMLIN. Moscow 1966.

Donova, K.V.: THE TREASURES OF THE DIAMOND FUND (exhibition catalogue). Moscow 1967.

Zonova, O.: MONUMENTS OF RUSSIAN PAINTING FROM THE 12TH CENTURY. Moscow 1967.

Radshenko, B.: THE CLOCKS OF MOSCOW. Moscow 1967.

Tihomirov, N., and V. Ivanov: THE MOSCOW KREMLIN. HISTORY OF [ITS] ARCHITECTURE. Moscow 1967.

TREASURES OF THE DIAMOND FUND OF THE USSR. Moscow 1967.

Pomerantsev, N.: THE REVOLUTIONARY PEOPLE AND THEIR CULTURAL MONUMENTS. Moscow 1968.

PRESERVATION OF HISTORICAL AND CULTURAL MONUMENTS (1917–1918). In: SOVIET ARCHIVES 3, 1969.

Gontsharova, A., and A.M. Hamtsov: WALLS AND TOWERS OF THE KREMLIN. Moscow 1969.

Ilyin, M.: MOSCOW. Moscow 1970.

[GOING] THROUGH THE KREMLIN. Moscow 1970.

ANCIENT MONUMENTS IN THE MOSCOW KREMLIN. Moscow 1971 (in the series "Information and Research about the Architecture of Moscow").

Ivanov, V.: THE MOSCOW KREMLIN. Moscow 1971.

Feodorov, V.: THE MOSCOW KREMLIN AND THE RECONSTRUCTION OF THE CENTER. In: ARCHITECTURE OF THE USSR 6, 1971.

THE USPENSKII CATHEDRAL (OF THE ASSUMPTION) IN THE MOSCOW KREMLIN. Moscow 1971.

Zalikova, E.: THE OLD CATHEDRALS OF THE KREMLIN. Moscow 1972.

MOSCOW. ARCHITECTURAL MONUMENTS FROM THE 14TH–17TH CENTURIES. Accompanying text by M. Ilyin. Moscow 1973.

THE NATIONAL MUSEUMS OF THE MOSCOW KREMLIN. INFORMATION AND RESEARCH. Vol. 1, Moscow 1973; Vol. 2, 1976.

PRESERVATION OF HISTORICAL AND CULTURAL MONUMENTS. Moscow 1973.

HISTORY OF MOSCOW. Moscow 1974.

Feodorov, V.: AN OUTSTANDING MONUMENT OF INTERNATIONAL CULTURE. In: ENGINEERING AND ARCHITECTURE IN MOSCOW 11, 1974.

Shelyapina, N.: ARCHAEOLOGICAL RESEARCH INTO THE MOSCOW KREMLIN (OLD TOPOGRAPHY AND STRATIGRAPHY). Author's speech about his/her dissertation. Moscow 1974.

Blok, G.: MOSKOWLANYJE. Moscow 1975.

Markova, G.: THE GRAND KREMLIN PALACE. Moscow 1975.

Nikolayev, Ye.: CLASSICIST MOSCOW. Moscow 1975.

Pekareva, N.: THE KREMLIN'S PALACE OF CONGRESS. Moscow 1975.

Topolin, M.: THE KREMLIN STARS. Moscow 1975.

Feodorov, B.: THE MOSCOW KREMLIN. Leningrad 1975.

Nenarokomova: THE NATIONAL MUSEUMS OF THE MOSCOW KREMLIN. Moscow 1977.

Kultshinski, D.: PRESERVATION OF THE ARCHITECTURAL MONUMENTS OF THE MOSCOW KREMLIN. Moscow 1977.

Nenarokomova/Zizov, Je.: ART TREASURES OF THE NATIONAL MUSEUMS IN THE MOSCOW KREMLIN. Moscow 1978.

Gilarovski, V.A.: MOSCOW AND MUSCOVITES. Moscow 1979.

MEMORIES OF N. KRUPSKAIA. Moscow 1979.

Tolstaia, T.: THE USPENSKII CATHEDRAL (OF THE ASSUMPTION) IN THE MOSCOW KREMLIN. Moscow 1979.

500 YEARS OF THE USPENSKII CATHEDRAL (OF THE ASSUMPTION) IN THE MOSCOW KREMLIN. Results of an academic conference. Moscow 1979.

Badulina, I.: BLAGOVESHCHENSKII CATHEDRAL (OF THE ANNUNCIATION). Moscow 1980.

MOSCOW'S PANORAMA. ON SEVEN HILLS. Moscow 1980.

Duncan, David Douglas: THE KREMLIN. New York and Dusseldorf/Vienna 1980 (Reprint).

Zacharov, I.: THE KREMLIN CHIMES. Moscow 1980.

THE ARCHITECTS OF MOSCOW. Vol. 1 (15th – 19th Centuries). Edited by Yu. Yaralov. Moscow 1981.

Pissarevskaia, L., and I. Rodimzeva: THE MOSCOW KREMLIN. Moscow 1981.

Portnov, M.: THE TSAR CANNON AND THE TSAR BELL. Moscow 1982.

Slavina, T.: KONSTANTIN TON (THE ARCHITECTS OF OUR CITY). Leningrad 1982.

Rodimzeva, I.: KREMLIN. HISTORY OF THE ARCHITECTURE AND ART MONUMENTS IN THE MOSCOW KREMLIN IN 8 VOLUMES. Moscow 1982 ff. (Vol. 1).

Libson, V.: REBIRTH OF THE TREASURES OF MOSCOW. Moscow 1983.

MOSCOW. ILLUSTRATED HISTORY. Vol. 1 (until 1917). Moscow 1984.